B N
B s at 16

BE YOUR OWN BOSS at 16

Alan S Watts

KOGAN PAGE

Acknowledgement

The computer programmer's story on page 52 was provided by Lee Rodmell, and first appeared in *Family*, the TSB magazine.

First published in 1986 by
Kogan Page Ltd, 120 Pentonville Road, London N1 9JN

British Library Cataloguing in Publication Data
Watts, Alan S.
Be your own boss at 16.
1. Small business 2. Self-employed
I. Title
658'.041 HD62.7

ISBN 1-85091-041-3

Printed and bound in Great Britain by
Dotesios (Printers) Limited, Bradford-on-Avon, Wiltshire

Contents

Chapter 1

Working for Yourself

What an idea! To leave school and become your own boss right away! It is something not just to dream about, but to think about. Dreamers don't get far. Thinkers do. As a wise man once said 'Castles in the air are all right, provided you put foundations under them.' The castles in the air in this case are the ideas this book might give you. It is up to you to provide the foundations – the solid basis on which your business will have to stand. This book will give you guidance.

THE RESPONSIBILITIES

There are great advantages in working for yourself. You can use your own initiative and reap the financial rewards of putting your own ideas into practice. You can avoid the frustration of being turned down repeatedly while you are seeking an employer. With so much unemployment everywhere today, you know how difficult it is to get a job. Very few firms are expanding. Indeed the tendency is mainly the other way – work forces are being slashed as new methods increase productivity but swell the unemployment figures. If you can set up a little business of your own you will not have to go cap in hand to all the firms in your neighbourhood.

Being your own boss also brings a certain amount of freedom. But you would be wrong to imagine that you could do just as you liked. Much would depend on the sort of business you go into. In some cases you might be able to choose your own hours, and even decide to take a day off whenever you wish. But others demand almost all your time. If you become a newsagent, for example, you will not be able to lie in bed in the morning. The same applies if you become a fruiterer: you will need to be up early to get to the central market.

However, whether you are free to lie in bed or not, you *will* be your own boss. You will not depend on anyone's favour for promotion. You will not have to get anyone's permission to slip home early or have to plead for a particular fortnight for your summer holiday. You are also responsible to yourself and must not think you'll be free from supervision or criticism. People working for themselves have to satisfy their clients (as indeed do all suppliers of goods and services), but in a small business you are much nearer the client than in a large one. A self-employed window-cleaner can expect to be told off pretty sharply if the windows are not properly cleaned or if a flowerbed is damaged through the careless positioning of a ladder. In fact, a person doing housework may well come to wonder who is the real boss – him/herself or the lady of the house.

The truth is that if you are to be successful working on your own account, you have to be your own boss in a very real sense. You have to be (if you can imagine it) *two people*. The first person is yourself, *the worker*. The other is yourself, *the boss*. *The boss* has to see that *the worker* is a good timekeeper and performs the work satisfactorily. Both these people merge into one, but you must realise that two functions have to be performed. You forget this at your peril. Many young people fail because they have not 'bossed' themselves strictly enough.

THE UNCERTAINTIES

There are also disadvantages in working for yourself. You not only have to *do* the work, you have to find it. You may discover that it takes more time to gain clients than actually to carry out the jobs. When you have found work and built up some good contacts so that you have a market for whatever you have to offer, you must exert every effort to keep that market. This may not present many problems so long as things run smoothly. But what happens if, for example, you fall sick? If you are unable to leave your sick-bed for a week or two, you may lose a valuable customer – or even all your customers. The same might happen if you take a holiday. Obviously you have to make some contingency plans, if at all possible, to meet emergencies.

This responsibility is all on your shoulders. If you get a sore throat and runny nose and feel you really should have a day or two in bed, it is impossible for you to make someone else responsible for finding a substitute. Your commitments may well force you, ill as you may be, to go out into the rain and cold. It is up to you to see that your contracts are fulfilled.

You are also responsible for the financial side of your business. More will be said about this in Chapter 7, but you have to see that the bills are paid, that you are properly insured, that you can pay the wages of anyone you might employ, and that you can meet any liability.

Employed people have a lot done for them. This is not always realised, but it is as well to remember that an employer sees that National Insurance contributions are paid, and that income tax is deducted and given regularly to the Inland Revenue. An employer sees that his workers receive holidays with pay. If any of them report sick, he pays them sickness benefit for the first seven days without their having to go to the doctor for a sick note. A self-employed person has none of these advantages.

How Long Will the Work Last?

Another disadvantage is that the work often proves to be short-lived. In some types of occupation this is because of the very nature of the work. People who build or repair things cannot expect a particular job to go on for ever – unless, for example, they are employed to paint the Forth Bridge or maintain the electrical plant of a large building. Jobs like these, however, are most unlikely to come the way of a 16-year-old school-leaver. So if you set out to construct or repair things you must be ready to seek new work all the time.

Of course, there are many types of work which do not have this once-for-all character. If you take up baby-sitting you can expect that an engagement, even if for one night only every week, will continue for some while. If you go in for housework, you might reasonably expect that you will have a regular engagement once or twice a week for as long as you can foresee.

Yet even engagements which seem to be permanent have a habit of suddenly coming to an end. One of the housewives for whom you work might have to move to another district. Even if you are working at several other houses, the loss of this one might so reduce your income that it might be better for you financially if you became wholly unemployed.

Many self-employed people are engaged in very uncertain

work, especially if they are 'freelances'. So much depends, of course, on the occupation(s) they choose to follow. Later in this book there are examples of young people who have good prospects of continual employment for a long time ahead. But it must be realised that there are many others who are constantly having to find fresh work, and the strain of doing so can be very great.

THE FREELANCE WORKER

Working freelance for other people can be a fairly uncertain occupation and the problems of one houseworker, illustrated below, show how routines can be easily upset. Although it is important to stress the hazards of this type of work, it is equally true that there are opportunities for a steady income provided you work hard at establishing good relations with your clients.

The Experiences of a Houseworker

Rose can vouch for the strains of being a houseworker. She found it impossible to get work when she left school. She had no O levels to speak of, so she says. Actually she obtained two – in English and Domestic Science. She decided, after six months of very disheartening unemployment, that she would become a domestic help. The idea had nothing to do with her having a domestic science pass.

She now began to look about for work. She was surprised how many notices there were in the local shop windows. Lots of people (it was a fairly well-off suburban area) needed their houses or flats cleaning, and although some of the addresses were too far for Rose to walk to, and there were drawbacks to some of the other adverts, she was left with a number to choose from.

The very first householder whom Rose telephoned was keen to see her. From this response Rose gained the impression that, in her part of the world at any rate, domestic help was not easy to get. Or was it that the people who offered themselves for employment were unreliable?

She went to see the lady. Her house was a very pleasant one in one of the wealthier parts of the town. It was not a very large house, or family – merely the husband, wife, and teenage daughter.

The lady asked Rose a number of questions about herself. She was a little surprised when Rose said she was only 16, perhaps because Rose looks older. 'Just two years older than my Sally', she remarked. She wanted to know why Rose wished to take up housework. 'After all,' she said, 'you've been to a good school. Can't you get a job in a bank or somewhere?' Rose had to confess that her GCE results had been poor, at which the lady looked a little pitying. 'Then why don't you go into a shop, or a supermarket – or the engineering firm on the industrial estate?'

Rose began to wonder what all this had to do with engaging her for housework, but she answered all the questions as well as she could, and with good grace. At last, the lady said: 'I need to know that you are honest. I have a lot of nice things in the house.'

Rose said she had always been honest, had never stolen anything, and treated other people's property with respect. She felt a little hurt at being doubted, and added: 'My headmistress can vouch for me, and I can supply other references too. The vicar knows me well, and you can phone him if you like.'

The lady said she would, and asked to see the reference Rose had got from her school. It was agreed that, provided her references were satisfactory, Rose could start work on the following Wednesday. She would be required each Wednesday and Friday morning, and would be paid £12 plus her bus fares.

This was the start of Rose's self-employment. Within a fortnight she had obtained other cleaning jobs to fill in most of the remaining days. One of them involved meeting two children at the primary school, bringing them home, and looking after them until their parents returned from work at about 6 pm. She also acted as baby-sitter for this couple every Saturday evening. These jobs, put together, seemed to make a good week's work, and Rose was happy to have a satisfactory income at last.

But within a month things happened to upset the pattern. The father of the two children suddenly got notice to take up a post in South Africa. This meant that the whole family would have to move overseas, the wife giving up her own job to follow her husband. Although Rose's job did not come to an end immediately, it began to tail off. At the end of the school term, which came shortly after the news of the transfer, the children's mother decided to give up her job so that she could be with the girls during the holiday weeks before they flew to Johannesburg. Now Rose had only the Saturday evening employment from her as baby-sitter. This greatly reduced her income.

For some reason new jobs did not now seem so easy to get. Rose applied for one as a school cleaner and found there were lots of other applicants; she was not successful. She answered one or two other advertisements without success and began to think that her days of self-employment were coming to an end. When she was offered evening work in the restaurant part of a large public house, she felt it was too good an offer to refuse. So she took it, although it meant the end of her baby-sitting jobs. She was, however, able to carry on with her housework engagements.

The strain of finishing an afternoon's house cleaning and going almost at once to the public house soon began to tell, however. So she reorganised her day work so that she would have all the afternoons free and be able to rest and enjoy some leisure hours. But as a result she has to admit that she is no longer fully self-employed and her social life is almost nil because the restaurant is open seven nights a week. She is therefore looking for some extra day work to enable her to give up the evening work altogether or reduce it to one or two evenings a week.

Facing Up to Difficulties

The problems faced by Rose are not confined to people working in domestic service. All who give a service are likely to meet similar difficulties. They might also find that they are no longer required after a while because some rival has undercut them or is able to offer a wider range of services. This is not such a danger for people who have built up a close relationship with the clients who give them work; loyalty to each other can preserve business ties. But a 16-year-old newcomer has to work hard for the chance to show such loyalty.

The importance of gaining a reputation for this quality must be emphasised. Gardeners and window-cleaners, for example, could often be replaced by others who seem to be cheaper, more skilled, more reliable etc. If they themselves are always keen to leave one person's service and find what they think are better jobs, they are at risk of being discarded themselves without much compunction. But there are many people who retain their jobs because their employer has felt: 'Well, they've come here in all sorts of weather, and although they mightn't be the very best workers you could find, at least they're reliable and honest. It would be disloyal to give the contract to someone else.'

Personal Relationships

Good personal relationships are most important, especially if you are performing a personal service for someone. It is the easiest thing in the world to come to loggerheads with the people you are working for. Housewives, for example, are apt to have particular ways of doing things. These are not always the most logical or sensible ways, but they stick to their cherished method or time-hallowed routine with a grim lack of reason. They expect their domestic helps to follow their instructions to the letter, to replace everything in its proper receptacle, the right way up, and in the correct order. So the domestic help ought to be aware when encountering housewives of this sort that danger threatens.

Friction can easily undermine friendly relations. The continuance of a job may very well depend on the worker's tact. And let's face it, when you are 16 you are not always as tactful as you might be. You might not even realise you have rubbed someone up the wrong way. So it is not merely a matter of being tactful, it is important to be *sensitive* also. You have to develop a set of antennae to detect early signs of having said (or done) the wrong thing. You must then quickly spot the cause of the trouble and put it right, with apologies:

'Oh, Mrs X! I am so sorry I didn't change into my slippers when I came in. I'll do it right away.'

STARTING A BUSINESS

These last examples may give the impression that all self-employed people work in domestic service, gardening, window-cleaning, or something of that sort. In Chapter 4 there are many examples of other sorts of work, and indeed this book is mainly concerned with young people in businesses of their own, and not working freelance for others.

Let us now consider setting up your own business, however small it may be. A business differs from freelancing in that the person operating a business has to buy, sell, move, or manufacture something. It is truly self-employment, because no one else employs you apart from yourself – no housewife, magazine editor, office manager etc.

One of the most encouraging developments in the last few years has been the rise in the number of small businesses. These contribute a great deal to the nation's well-being. There are around 1,300,000 of them. Some employ up to 100 people, but the majority are two- or three-person concerns, such as small shops, jobbing builders, restaurants, boarding-houses, and so on. They account for about one person in every three employed in the private sector (that is, outside the civil service, local authorities, police, teachers, health service, and all the various public utilities and nationalised industries). Altogether they produce about one-fifth of the country's net income.

Thousands of jobs have been lost in all the big industries on which we have customarily relied for employment. There have been massive redundancies in steel works, mines, shipyards and railways. In fact, almost all the new jobs which have been created have been in small businesses. No wonder the government wants to help them and has set up agencies to offer advice and assistance to small-business people. Details of these are given later in Chapter 8.

Having said that, a word of warning is necessary. School-leavers are likely to be discouraged when they read the various pamphlets and leaflets distributed by these agencies. They will find no direct reference to assistance provided for young people such as themselves. The help being offered is mainly to older people who have a fair amount of capital behind them, or sufficient expertise and experience to make the raising of capital no insuperable problem. When the official literature talks about 'small businessmen', it is often referring to employers of several staff units – even as many as 100. 'Small' is a matter of degree.

Use Information to Your Advantage

Still, it is a good thing to read as much about small businesses as possible. Businesses begin as ideas, and many of the really big ones of today started off as quite simple ideas. You can begin to pick up hints from the many articles which appear in the business press describing new developments, the history of firms, and the success of entrepreneurs. (This word 'entrepreneur' is one you might not have come across before. But you will read it again and again in books and articles dealing with setting up new businesses. It means a person who begins a business enterprise – an 'enterpriser'.)

When you read these articles, at first you may be disappointed. Often the information given and the ideas floated are not of much use to 16-year-olds at first glance. But because an idea cannot be adopted directly, it doesn't mean that it is a useless one. Very often the principle can be developed to suit your own circumstances. For example, there was a newspaper report recently about a successful small business which purchased surplus machine tools for resale. It would be quite impossible for a school-leaver to start such a business: it would need considerable capital and involve providing transport and storage facilities. But the idea of buying surplus goods and reselling them is excellent. Anyone who has seen a London street market knows that most of the goods offered for sale there have been bought as surplus stock. When the big stores bring out a new line, they often have considerable stocks of old goods to clear. They sell them off to small traders.

The majority of these traders are regular stall-holders. There are, however, many 'irregular' traders who don't have stalls. You can see them with their open suitcases balanced on upturned boxes or something similar, offering reasonably priced articles such as briefs, T-shirts or blouses to people passing by.

GETTING A BUSINESS MIND

Another good reason for reading books and articles on small businesses is to get 'small-business minded'. Even if the small businesses you read about have capital assets running into thousands of pounds and employ 60 or 70 people, their problems might well be your problems, and their triumphs might well show you a way to similar ones.

If you are really keen on being your own boss at 16, you must expect to continue being your own boss when you are 26, 36, and so on. You want to be business minded from the start. This is perhaps where we, as a nation, fail. Napoleon is said to have called us a nation of shopkeepers, that is, of small businessmen. But we are not really. Most of us are by nature *employees*. When we leave school all our energies are directed towards finding someone to give us a job. If we cannot find that someone we are at a loss to know what to do.

However, this is not the case with every section of our community. For example, people from the Indian sub-continent have quite a different attitude. They are not 'born employees' like most of the rest of us; they are 'born small businessmen'. Their natural instinct is to start a business for themselves or take over an existing one. Many corner shops, pharmacies and sub-post offices have been acquired by this section of our community. They are prepared to work hard, endure long hours, and plough back their profits to expand their businesses. They are a group of people who deserve our admiration and from whom we can learn a great deal. The fact that they have taken over so many small businesses shows how reluctant other groups in the community have been to do so, and how 'employee-minded' most of us are.

A recent article in *The Times* drew attention to the lack of any tradition in the north east of England of people starting their own businesses. The working population has always been mainly employed in textiles, coal-mining, iron and steel manufacture and shipbuilding. Now that these industries are declining there is not sufficient work with employers to go round. So it is most important to try and encourage people to start on their own. Yet even fewer than in other parts of the country have ever given a moment's thought to it.

With these problems in mind, a scheme, 'Education for Enterprise', has been started at several comprehensive schools. Their aim is to get young people 'own-business minded'. Some classes in these schools have actually set up little businesses making and selling such things as sweets, jewellery and toys. Their main purpose, however, is to change attitudes and encourage self-reliance, so that people might escape from the traditional dependence on big firms to provide them with jobs.

Project North East has helped to get started 86 businesses which have given work to 119 young people. There are 15 businesses in the centre's premises with others outside, including a sports shop.

The intention is to provide young business people with workshop space, advice, common facilities and access to finance. The facilities include telephones and an answering service, while a loan fund is being set up with the backing of the Prince's Trust Youth Business Initiative and the Young Enterprise Scheme.

The Failure Rate for Small Businesses

It would be wrong to conceal the fact that there is a big turnover in small businesses. It is said that many of the 170,000 founded every year should never have been started at all – the figures show that about 120,000 collapse every year. There is, therefore, a gradual increase in the number of small businesses, but it is not as high as it might be. Some of the reasons why businesses fail will come out in the course of this book.

Find the Right Area

It should be pointed out that some parts of the country are more favourable for small businesses and freelance activities than others. Jobbing builders are more likely to be required in a stockbroker belt than in an area of high unemployment where most people live in council houses and can probably do any building work themselves. Houseworkers and gardeners are in much greater demand in suburbia than city centres. When planning to start a business you must take full account of the conditions in which it will operate.

Find the Right Service

It has been said above that many businesses should never have been started at all. But it has also been said that there are many businesses which should be started, but have not been.

What businesses should have been started? We must use our imagination to find out. We might regret that our great grandfather was so stupid as not to realise that a road-side garage would become a great money-spinner as motor transport increased. We have thus been deprived of a lucrative inheritance. But we would probably be wrong to assume that technological developments now taking place give us similar opportunities. Most of them would require massive amounts of capital and considerable expertise in advanced electronics. This is not to say that there are not many small firms specialising in advanced electronic work. Few school-leavers are, however, equipped to enter this field.

Examples of businesses which were waiting to be started are the Little Chef restaurant chain, Smith's potato crisps, and Initial Services providing clean towels to office workers. There must be several others. They began as bright ideas, required only moderate capital to get under way, and once started they rapidly expanded.

It is up to you to keep your eyes and minds open to discover a service or a product which is needed but not at present provided. It is said that the best ideas are the simple ones. This may not help you to think one up, but it may warn you that what you are looking for is so simple that this is the reason why everyone has overlooked it. What idea could be more simple than providing towels for office workers?

On the other hand, the business which is really needed might not be one providing a new product or service; it might be one which gives an existing service or sells an existing product but at some place which lacks these facilities. There are still places with no tea-shop within miles, others with no typewriter repairer. People sometimes search in vain for a shop selling ordinary pieces of ironmongery such as screws, nuts, bolts, hinges, or mousetraps. So go out and see how easy or difficult it is to get a whole range of items which you reckon must be needed by your neighbours.

Find the Right Attitude

A recent series of articles in a Sunday newspaper stressed the fact that 'business is for the bold'. This is true. The main reason we tend to be 'employees' is that we lack the courage to strike out for ourselves. Boldness, however, does not mean recklessness. Courage in founding a business must be accompanied by caution, and caution implies taking all available advice and learning the fundamentals.

In 1984 Edinburgh Venture Enterprise Trust initiated a competition to encourage awareness of the commercial world among senior pupils who were invited to form mini-companies within their schools, appointing their own boards of directors and management, and deciding on a product or a service. They raised money by issuing share capital so that pupils and teachers could buy a maximum of ten 50p shares. The companies were required to keep proper books of account to record their transactions, and to aim to make a profit and pay a dividend.

Business is also for the hard-working. No doubt one has to have a flair for business, the ability to see opportunities and seize them at the right time. But flair is not enough. In most businesses, a lot of hard work over long hours is required.

The important thing if you contemplate working for yourself is to go into it with your eyes open. It is not an easy form of employment, but it can be a very rewarding one.

Chapter 2

What Can I Do?

While you were at school you probably had some careers advice, either from your careers guidance teacher or a careers officer. Careers advice normally follows a set pattern. First the adviser tries to help you discover what sort of a person you are and where your interests and abilities lie.

Only when you have a reasonably clear picture of yourself and have stopped day-dreaming about glamour jobs for which you are quite unsuited can you weigh up practical possibilities and choices.

DO YOU HAVE THE ESSENTIAL QUALITIES?

If you are thinking of working for yourself you need to be sure you are the sort of person who is likely to be successful. What sort of a person do you have to be? Here are a few basic requirements:

1. You Must be Healthy

Health is an important requirement in all jobs, but especially so for those working on their own account. So many of these jobs are physically demanding – house-cleaning, decorating, lawn-mowing, delivering papers, window-cleaning etc. They can only be done by healthy, robust people. They often involve standing for long periods and being out of doors in all sorts of weather. Some of them need considerable muscle and the ability to lift heavy weights.

There are other points to bear in mind, too. It was emphasised in the last chapter that when you are your own boss absence through sickness can lose you valuable customers. With everything relying on you yourself, you cannot afford days off. Sickness can lead to the business you have so painfully built up going to pieces very rapidly.

2. You Must be Outgoing

You might imagine that some jobs don't need outgoing people at all. Gardeners, for instance, seem to be reflective people, concerned with their own thoughts as they dig and hoe. But if they are to work for themselves, seeking jobs at a number of houses to make up a full week's work, they need to talk to people, mix with neighbours who might help, and generally assert their personalities. A certain amount of 'pushiness' is needed to discover and take advantage of opportunities. Shy retiring souls may have excellent qualifications and they may possess great skill, but unless they can get out and sell themselves, they are hardly likely to get very far. In fact, they would be better advised to seek employment in someone else's enterprise. On the other hand, the good mixers, the chatterboxes, the people who take an interest in other people and their affairs, are the ones who thrive when working on their own account.

3. You Must be Mentally Alert

Great academic ability is not a basic requirement. People can succeed in being their own boss without having many, or even any, O or A level passes. Mental alertness and academic ability are not the same thing. The stock figure of the absent-minded professor is not just a comic invention but an example of how qualifications do not always mean sharpness. On the other hand, there are many young people whose scholastic record is rather poor, but who are very observant, sharp-witted and quick to take hold of ideas.

The differences between academic and natural ability were highlighted by the experiences of a young man who left a public school with three good A level passes. He decided that before going to university he would take a job in the accounts branch of a large firm. There he found himself working with people who had nothing like his academic attainments, or any interest in the sort of areas he had been educated in. They didn't care about art, books, the theatre, ballet, or anything like that. Their conversation was mainly about the football results, TV programmes, and their cars. A lot of their working time was spent trying to pick the winners of horse-races, and during their lunch break they would call at the betting office on their way to the pub. The young public-school boy found himself in quite an alien world.

However, what amazed him was the sharp awareness of his new colleagues. They had a marvellous skill in mental calculations: they could reckon up their winnings from the bookmaker (when they had any) with wonderful speed. They also possessed a detailed knowledge of London bus routes, taxi fares, the prices of second-hand cars and motorcycles, the best places to buy wallpaper and paint, and a host of other things. Their young colleague had to express his admiration for them. He felt he had been taught very few immediately useful things at school, while the others had not only become well versed in practical matters, but had developed far quicker wits.

This example is not intended to show that schooling and higher education are unimportant – indeed they are. The point it makes is that people who have not shone at school may none the less be very bright and mentally alert, and these qualities are essential if you are to work for yourself.

ANALYSE YOURSELF FURTHER

Let us assume you decide you have these three basic qualities. You now want to find out what other qualities and abilities you possess, and having done that, how you can put them to the best use. You must be perfectly honest with yourself, noting down what you can do, and whether you can do them well or merely passably, and then deciding what you can't do or are very poor at. You may be surprised at what skills you possess.

Most of us – even if we confess we are not perfect – believe we are pretty good. So it is hard to answer questions like these honestly. We might not see ourselves as others see us, but we must try. Our strengths and weaknesses have a great bearing on our work, whether we work for ourselves or for an employer. If you work for an employer he or she may well have to tell you about your shortcomings. But if you work for yourself you must rely on honest self-examination.

Here are the various headings under which you might examine yourself:

Personality

You have already decided you are outgoing. You believe you get on well with other people. But are there any types of person you get on with best. Children? Young people? Housewives? Men? The elderly?

At 16 you probably have the best relationships with those of your own age. You share similar interests, talk the same jargon, enjoy the same jokes. Yet you may also be very good with babies and young children, for example. Through your experiences going shopping you might share many of the feelings – frustration, enjoyment, triumph – felt by older shoppers, and be able to talk to them sympathetically and helpfully. You might get on well with motorists, particularly with car buffs. On the other hand you might realise you have serious limitations when it comes to dealing with technical people. You might know that if you had to give advice at a do-it-yourself shop you could never face up to the type of customers you would be likely to meet. Then again, you might enjoy the company of the sort of customer you would meet in a city pub. It can be useful to know where you would best fit in.

Remember, however, that you will develop. A school-leaver is usually a fish out of water in his or her first job. Yet within weeks a change has taken place. The awkward school-leaver has rapidly adapted to the new surroundings and become acquainted with new companions. The young person who felt unable to handle or chat confidently with certain types of person, is actually doing so, easily and skilfully. In analysing oneself, allowance must be made for such development.

You should also look at other aspects of your personality and consider whether they might have any bearing on your working on your own account. Ask yourself, are you patient or quick-tempered? When you undertake a job do you think it over calmly and take trouble over the preparations for it, or do you dash at it recklessly? You may be excellent at talking nicely to customers, but are you able to work alongside others without friction? Do you get annoyed with people helping you because their methods aren't yours, or because they are a little on the slow side? Do you ever rub people up the wrong way? Have you ever thought why?

Academic Ability

You have decided you are mentally alert, but how good are you at academic subjects? What did you like doing at school? How is your English? Can you write a good grammatical letter? Can you spell? Do you know how to set out a business letter? Can you type it accurately? If you can't type, can you write in a good clear hand?

Then, what about mathematics? Can you do simple arithmetic – adding, subtracting, multiplying and dividing? What about working out interest rates and percentages? Are you confident you can handle fractions and decimals? Do you use a pocket calculator, and can you do more complicated calculations on it than mere addition and division? What about more advanced mathematics? Have you any skill at geometry or trigonometry? Do you consider yourself really *numerate*?

Both English and maths are important subjects for any businessman. Unless you are in a very small concern indeed, you will have to write letters and plan ahead, making various calculations to forecast your inflow and outflow of money and sorting out taxes and National Insurance. Some types of work may make a considerable demand on your arithmetic – working out the volume of materials you will require for particular jobs, their cost and the price you will have to charge your customer.

Special Academic Interests

You may not, however, see how other academic subjects can have a bearing on being your own boss at 16. What use, you might ask, could history be, or geography? But if you have been keenly interested in a subject the fact is worth noting. For example, people with a strong interest in history or geography might make excellent guides, and they will certainly get along well with people who are similarly curious.

There is a shopkeeper in a picturesque, historic little town in the north of England. He sells postcards, souvenirs, and various bric-à-brac. His wife also provides morning coffee and afternoon tea. They do extremely well, mainly perhaps because of his keen interest in that locality.

He talks in a friendly way to everyone coming into the shop, finds out if they are walkers or motorists, and whether they are familiar with the district. He has accurate information about the historic places in the vicinity, and tells people how they can get there and what to look for on the way. His interest in local geography and history is really a part of his stock in trade, as it helps him greatly in selling postcards and toasted teacakes. Tourists so enjoy coming into his shop and talking with him that they not only come again but tell their friends about him when they return home.

Academic interests can often be made to serve you in whatever work you take up. And, of course, they can often point the way to a particular job. So your self-examination should not overlook any ability or interest, however irrelevant it might seem at first sight.

Creative Ability

Many people have been able to start little businesses of their own through their ability to create. We all probably have some creative ability, but do not recognise it because we are not fine artists. So it is wrong to assume you are lacking in this respect – it may be the basis for your own business.

First of all, however, let us consider the more artistic forms of creativity. Did you take art at school, and did you gain any O levels or other qualifications? How good are you at drawing or painting? Have you carried out any decorative work such as painting on china, lettering, or marquetry? Have you done any designing, such as dress-designing, wallpaper or fabric patterns, or display? Have you done any pottery, or any other form of three-dimensional art? What about toy-making, dressmaking, or soft-furnishing?

There are several other activities closely related to artistic creation. You might have abilities in graphic design, engineering drawing, photography, or film-making.

Your talents can also take quite different forms, such as woodwork and metalwork. You probably did one or the other at school – how suited were you for such work? You may have had some creative hobby – did you ever construct model aeroplanes, yachts, battle-scenes etc? Have you tinkered with radios?

Perhaps you are interested in cookery – have you practised it at home or school? Cookery must come high on the list as a skill which can be turned into self-employment. It is worth working at, and developing a deeper interest in. If you have an artistic temperament and flair for decoration, these can be coupled most usefully with your culinary skill. A good restaurant calls for more than a good chef; it has to have attractive premises, with pleasing décor. Well-set tables and artistically arranged flowers contribute to the atmosphere which gives a restaurant its particular appeal to customers.

Mechanical Ability

Many people are not at all artistic, but they have a flair for understanding mechanics. There is usually an element of creative ability in their make-up as well.

Are you a mechanically minded person? Can you take things to pieces and put them together again? Do you like tinkering with engines, not minding if you get your hands covered in oil? Do you ever think how you might improve the performance of your motorbike? Think about developing these interests.

You may have picked up some scientific or technical knowledge, perhaps at school or through your hobbies. Such familiarity could be very useful. For instance, an understanding of elementary magnetism or electricity will give you some idea of how electric motors work, and these are the basis of all sorts of domestic appliances: vacuum cleaners, food mixers, lawn-mowers, electric clocks and fans, hair-dryers etc. A basic knowledge of electricity will also give some clue about the workings of electrical systems in motor vehicles.

Another branch of mechanics is the use of engineering tools. Perhaps you have some experience here. You may have shaped pieces of metal by drilling and filing them, or been taught how to operate the micrometer and vernier for measuring very small dimensions and working to fine limits.

At school you may have been introduced to machine tools and instructed in the working of a lathe. This training might be extremely useful to you. Suppose you set up a little workshop on your own account, you may not at first be able to equip it with expensive machine tools. But if the business prospers (remember how Lord Nuffield, then William Morris, founder of Morris Motors, began as a bicycle repairer) you would want to extend your scope. Training in machine tools, even if it had to be updated in the light of developments, would be invaluable.

If you have any training in electronics then you could think about developing this skill. Are you familiar with the basic theory of electronics, about semi-conductors, valves and integrated circuits? Do you know anything about the way radios and televisions work? More topically, you may have had some experience with computers and word processors at school – are you interested in programming and the various languages? As a result of the drive to make young people familiar with computers, most of you will have had some experience of this new technology. Some of you will be able to apply this knowledge and the skills you have attained to form a basis for a business of your own. Indeed, there are young people who have done this very successfully. It is a field in which young people have the edge over their elders.

Practical Ability

You may find that your main abilities are neither creative nor mechanical. You are a practical person. You can lay bricks, construct a concrete path, cultivate tomato plants, paper a room, get the stains out of carpets or bath babies.

Practical people with abilities such as these are often the best equipped to start a business of their own. Most of the jobs which are available and need to be done (such as repair work, cleaning, tidying and moving), are mundane practical ones. There are more details of these in the next chapter.

Some of this work does require some training and experience. You cannot very well offer to replace someone's broken window-pane without having some instruction in glazing. But much of it is within the range of completely inexperienced people.

Many people have practical abilities without realising it. They take them for granted. When asked what they can do, they tend to reply very weakly: 'Well, I can't really do anything.' But if they are questioned closely, all sorts of abilities come to light. Assess what skills or knowledge you possess. At school you might have picked up quite a lot of know-how through looking after the school's flat, or the school garden. Many of you have worked with your parents either in their business or about the house. Membership of a scout troop or guide company can result in the acquisition of all sorts of skills and knowledge. Not only are you encouraged to get proficiency badges for particular activities, but you learn by carrying out tasks for the group – caulking a boat, painting a hut etc.

It is up to you to question yourself. You may be doing something every day as a matter of routine, and not realise you have a talent which could be the basis of self-employment.

Administrative Ability

Businesses have to be administered, regardless of size. Even if you are engaged in a simple job such as window-cleaning, you must keep an account of what you earn or you will have problems with the Inland Revenue. More complex businesses require more administration. If you buy and sell goods you will have dealings with wholesalers; you will probably get goods on credit, and may allow your customers credit too. So you will have to keep careful accounts. You will also want to be ready to show how profitable your business is in the event of having to seek a loan to expand. As your business grows, you will have to spend more and more time on organisation.

Administration is not normally a school subject, but while you were there you might very well have had some suitable experience. Perhaps you were placed in charge of the library and had to keep a record of borrowings. Or you might have had to do more complicated tasks in the organisation of sports and athletics. If you have arranged an outing by motor coach then you will have had to take bookings and account for money entrusted to you. There are all sorts of ways in which you might have had to administer something which involved setting up records, keeping books, opening files, and so on.

If you have had this sort of responsibility you will know whether you enjoyed it or hated it, whether you found you were good, or whether you made a horrible mess of it. If administration is not your forte, you should not think of becoming involved in any business which depends for its success on good organisation and record-keeping.

Administration also involves the handling of staff. It is highly unlikely that you will find yourself an employer at 16, but you may have started on a path which will lead you to becoming one in a few years' time. Once you begin to employ other people you need administrative ability of a rather different sort. You have to be able to manage staff, and get them to work for you efficiently and without friction. This requires powers of leadership.

Already you may be sure you have such qualities if you have been captain of football or hockey, or been placed in charge of a platoon of the cadet corps. But leadership of this sort is not quite the same as leadership in a business. Management of staff is not just a matter of giving orders or instructing people, for you may find that your staff know much more about the job than you do – it is often a matter of tact and being sympathetic to the needs and problems of others. At times, however, you might have to be quite tough. If any of your staff are incompetent you may have to get rid of them. Some employers, especially in small businesses, find this extremely difficult to do.

It is difficult to assess your capabilities as a manager. If you can judge how tactful you are, and how forceful, you will have some idea. But for a beginning, you will probably only have one person to manage – yourself – and the question you must ask yourself now is whether you are self-disciplined enough to organise yourself properly.

ARE YOUR PRESENT ABILITIES SUFFICIENT?

When you have assessed yourself under these various headings, you ought to have some idea what you are capable of, and whether you are fitted for attempting to start out on your own account.

Let us assume you come to the conclusion that you do in fact possess real abilities. The question you must now ask yourself is whether these abilities are enough on their own. You may be excellent at tinkering with your own motorcycle, but could you take the responsibility of offering to repair someone else's when it is a different size and make? Do you need some specialised training?

Although some forms of work need no training at all, the great majority do. Even houseworkers have to be trained. A competent home-help is not only acquainted with the uses of domestic appliances – such as washing-machines, vacuum cleaners, polishers, cookers, microwave ovens – but should be able to prepare a variety of meals, and have some knowledge of hygiene and nutrition.

If you decide you need further training, how can you get it?

There are several ways. One is to work for a while with someone who can teach you. Another is to read the subject up; get books out of the public library, buy the appropriate technical journals. A better way still is to take a course, either full time, part time, or in the evenings, at a college of further education. This might delay your move into business, but it will ensure your being more successful when you do.

An excellent form of experience is to go into partnership with someone who possesses expertise from which you can learn. Your parents might be the obvious partners, otherwise you might find another older person. As you cannot have a driving licence until you are 17, entering into a partnership with someone who can provide transport and at the same time teach you what you feel you have yet to know about the business, can be a fruitful arrangement.

Chapter 3

Ideas for Self-Employment

It is surprising how much needs to be done all around us. Next time you are sitting in a railway carriage, look out of the window and observe what a tremendous amount of work ought to be carried out. Both on the railway line and private property lying alongside it, one can see mile after mile of decay and dilapidation. Land, buildings and equipment seem to have been left to go to ruin. Here and there a railwayman has been permitted to cultivate a small allotment by the side of the lines, but there is room for hundreds more. Girders and pieces of steel lie rusting in the rank grass. Buildings have their windows smashed. Piles of bricks are left to gather moss.

If you questioned the authorities and suggested they did something to restore or utilise the waste land, you would be told it isn't worth their while, the bottom has fallen out of the market, the present state of the economy doesn't allow it, and so on. No doubt all this is true, but the point of making these observations is to show that there is no shortage of jobs to be done. What you have seen from the railway carriage is only a tiny bit of Great Britain. If you could see the whole of the country you would realise what an immense amount of work is waiting for somebody and, in the hands of private individuals, it would not be subject to the sort of considerations which worry railway boards and industrialists.

REALISING THE OPPORTUNITIES

If you stay aware of your surroundings and what other people are saying then you may pick up some ideas, so take a walk through your own district. Go up and down the roads, along the alley-ways at the rear of houses, and through the industrial estates. Keep your eyes and ears open, and take a notebook to record what you see and hear.

Notes on an Afternoon's Walk

Here are some notes made during quite a short stroll in a suburban residential district:

No 4 The Parade – lawn overgrown. Fence between No 4 and No 6 rotten, several boards want replacing.
No 6 The Parade – garden tools left out and gone rusty.
No 11 Elder Avenue – car badly needs cleaning.
No 86 High Street – parking square used for displaying cars for sale needs sweeping out.
No 19 Lowther Road – gutter overflowing and water running down wall.
No 42 Lowther Road – windows very dirty.
Municipal Park – St Saviour's cricket-club's pavilion badly in need of painting.
No 18 Harold Way – goldfish pond wants cleaning out.
No 22 Harold Way – driveway muddy, requires new layer of gravel.
No 31 Harold Way – piles of builder's rubbish at side of house need removing.
No 14 Meadow Lane – garden a wilderness. Branches of shrubs make it difficult to walk up path, rose bushes in a tangle.
No 17 Meadow Lane – fallen trees need sawing into logs.

Hearing about Difficulties

It is a strange thing but many people have problems and difficulties and never take any step to solve them. Doctors are constantly coming across patients who have endured some discomfort for years and never thought of mentioning it. Just as people gossip about their ailments, they talk about their problems, and often use them as excuses for avoiding having to do something. They complain about not being able to get out for an evening because of their children, or because they are looking after an elderly relative. They complain about the size of their houses, and the difficulty they have in cleaning them. They moan about the amount of ironing they have to do, and how hard it is to find someone who will mow the lawn. Those who secretly enjoy being martyrs may be difficult to help, but you should keep your ears open for these complaints. Offer to help them – they might have to find a reliable baby-sitter or a conscientious houseworker. There is work here if they will let you have it.

Other people deplore the non-existence of certain types of trader. 'It used to be nice when there was a fishmonger in the High Street. But now if we want any fresh fish we have to go all the way to Westchester.' Or you might overhear people complaining about the rows of estate agents and building societies when they would like to browse through a second-hand bookshop.

Listening to people's complaints is a good way of discovering the needs of individuals and the local community. Whether you wish to set up a business or provide personal services on a freelance basis, you will gain lots of information merely by talking to people and listening.

Advertisements

Advertisements for part-time jobs such as baby-sitting, housework and gardening etc usually appear in shop windows. You should scan these displays regularly, making a note of any which seem to offer you suitable employment. Don't delay in following them up, but telephone as soon as you return home or reach a public call-box, unless the notice plainly says to get in contact after a certain time.

Be polite and enthusiastic. Be sympathetic, too. 'Yes. I quite understand your difficulties, and I'm sure I can help. It must be very awkward for you. But if I could bring in some of the shopping for you – if you left me a list, for example – you could be home sooner, couldn't you?' Tact, sympathy, and willingness are tremendous assets in getting and keeping this sort of job.

You should also keep your eye on local newspapers. They often (especially the free ones) carry adverts for people to distribute newspapers and leaflets. They also advertise for helpers in a surprisingly wide range of activities. For example, in a recent issue of a weekly newspaper in Kent, there were requests for people who could do needlework, clean offices, pack goods at home, prepare lunches for directors' meetings, look after a garden with a swimming pool, and assemble lampshades.

STARTING OFF

It is quite possible to regard yourself as being your own boss by undertaking a variety of small jobs. In Chapter 1 there was an account of Rose's experiences. She had found a number of different jobs to do – principally housework and baby-sitting – and for a while these provided her with an adequate income. However, before long she encountered difficulties, and these were largely due to the fact that she was not her own boss in the fullest sense of the term; she was really an employee of a number of employers. So although she had a certain amount of freedom and the sense of working on her own account, she had by no means succeeded in starting her own business.

It is not easy to define freelance working and make a clear distinction between it and working for an employer, or between it and working in one's own business. The distinctions can be important, especially in the matter of National Insurance. Employed persons pay Class 1 contributions and may receive benefits which self-employed persons who pay Class 2 contributions are not entitled to.

Although Rose regarded herself as self-employed, she really took orders from a number of housewives who no doubt regarded her as their employee. Things would have been different if she had set up a cleaning business – perhaps in partnership with someone else – and called this business 'Miss Mop Cleaners', for example. The difference between Rose going out to do housework for a particular householder, and 'Miss Mop Cleaners' arriving to do it, would not perhaps be very noticeable. 'Miss Mop Cleaners', however, would be expected to bring the necessary equipment and probably enter into a formal contract with the householder, and there would be no doubt in anyone's mind that the householder was not the employer of the person sent to do the work.

The idea of founding 'Miss Mop Cleaners' had never occurred to Rose. Even if it had, there would have been several problems to overcome. She would have needed money (capital) to buy equipment. She would have required a light van to carry it in, and being under 16 she would have no driving licence.

Yet she could have overcome these difficulties had she tried. Her friend, Sally, is a capable driver and has the use of a second-hand Mini. Sally too is unemployed, and would have been available to join as a partner. Rose could have borrowed suitable cleaning equipment from her mother. Together the two girls would have had everything needed to set up 'Miss Mop Cleaners'. Whether it would have fared better than Rose working on her own is a matter of opinion, but with two partners working together and pooling their knowledge of local needs, they would have stood a good chance of building up a successful business.

Why then, hasn't Rose gone ahead and done this? Why does she continue to go out as a 'daily', while her friend Sally lives on supplementary benefit? The reason, as Rose acknowledges, is that neither of them possesses the necessary enterprise.

Enterprise

You have been introduced already to the word 'entrepreneur'. It was defined as a person who begins an enterprise – an 'enterpriser'. It also means a person who has 'business enterprise'.

Enterprise is the active power which gets a business off the ground. You might have an excellent original idea. You might have all the necessary skills to put the idea into practice. You might have sufficient capital, even suitable premises (your own home, for instance), and yet nothing happens. You lack enterprise.

Many people boast of having ideas which other people have later taken up and developed. You may overhear remarks such as: 'I said to my wife many a time that what was needed along the roads was a string of moderately priced restaurants. You never knew whether those funny old tea-shoppes and farmhouse kitchens were any good, or how long they'd take to serve you.' Yet the people who now claim such intelligent foresight never had the inspiration to do anything about it. A person with enterprise (an entrepreneur) is ready to be bold, take a risk, show initiative and set out on an adventure. Founding a business is not for the faint-hearted.

SIMPLE BUSINESSES

Not every business needs a lot of capital, or involves the employment of other people. Many people conduct one-person businesses from their own homes. They do not actually perform the work at home in every case but they use home as their base.

Here are some ideas for home-based businesses. Some of them might verge on being freelance work for several employers, but others are clearly businesses where you will be working for yourself.

Cleaning

Some young people have moved from house cleaning to office cleaning. They are in competition, of course, with large firms of office cleaners, but they have opportunities to win contracts which the larger firms do not regard as economic. Suburban districts have many small offices belonging to estate agents, solicitors, surveyors, finance companies, and similar firms. All these offices need to be cleaned, and in many cases their occupants would rather have the work done by people they know and can trust than leave it in the hands of unknown employees of large firms.

It must be recognised that most of these offices are already being cleaned quite satisfactorily. It is no easy task to get a foothold in the business. You have to canvass the area, leaving your leaflets, and be especially enterprising wherever you see a new office block being erected. You should find out who has applied for tenancies and go and see them even before they move in.

It is not unusual for a firm to become exasperated by the poor standard of cleaning being performed. When staff complain repeatedly that their desks are never dusted properly, and the toilets and washbowls are neglected, a boss is compelled to look around for a replacement for the present cleaning contractor. You never know when this state of affairs exists, so it is as well to keep on delivering handbills as widely as you think fit.

Chimney Sweeping

It is a surprise to discover that there are young people actually engaged in this occupation when fewer chimneys need sweeping nowadays, and those which do are not as soot-laden as they used to be before smokeless fuel replaced coal. However, open fireplaces are becoming increasingly popular, so the demand for the services of chimney sweeps may well increase also. The flues of central heating systems also have to be cleaned every once in a while, and many industrial plants have flues and extraction plants which need attention. It is necessary to work with an experienced sweep before setting out on your own, and then you will require the essential equipment – machine or brushes.

Home Services

An interesting development in recent years has been the emergence of firms which will take on all sorts of domestic work. They will not only do cleaning, including shampooing carpets and laundering curtains, but will sand and polish floors, clean windows, look after lawns, repair fencing and flush drains. They are of great benefit to elderly people living on their own. Some of them will come and do the weekly wash, using the client's washing machine perhaps and ironing various articles afterwards.

The scope of these firms is often very wide, and some of the services which the larger ones provide are out of the question for a 16-year-old beginner. But this is the sort of business which could be started and expanded as time goes on.

Many of the firms have contracts with offices, shops and factories, so much of the work must be done in the evening or overnight. This is something to bear in mind if the idea of such a business attracts you.

Window-cleaning

Although this is one of the tasks which home services firms will undertake, there are many freelance workers who specialise in it. A newcomer to window-cleaning has to break into the existing system; it can be very disheartening trying to do so. The majority of householders are quite satisfied with their existing window-cleaner, and would be prejudiced against employing one who had just left school.

The best chance of finding work is with the occupants of new houses. Keep your eyes open for new estates being erected. As they are completed, call and see the new occupiers, or leave your advertising material. Persistence pays.

You need ladders and small items of equipment for this job and, as some form of transport is really essential, it may be better at first to go into partnership with someone a little older than yourself who can assist with a van. You also need to take advice about insurance; there are risks in window-cleaning, both to yourself and others. You should make sure you are adequately covered should an accident happen.

Window-cleaning is not an easy business to break into at any age, and is especially difficult for a school-leaver. But there are many young people making a good living out of it and finding that it offers opportunities for other types of work. Customers sometimes ask: 'While you are up there could you clean the leaves out of my gutters?' Whether most window-cleaners would be ready to oblige the lady who said there was a wasps' nest under her eaves and wanted someone to destroy it, is doubtful. However, there is no doubt that handy people with a set of ladders and who are used to working at heights, ought not to be short of jobs.

Typing and Duplicating

If you have achieved a reasonable degree of accuracy in your typing – speed will come with practice – you may think of offering to type authors' manuscripts and students' theses.

You will, of course, need a typewriter, and your best plan is to buy a good second-hand manual machine, but not a flimsy portable. Electric typewriters are excellent models, but unless you can afford to buy an expensive one, they are best avoided; cheap electric typewriters will not stand up to heavy use.

Typing manuscripts is not as easy as it sounds. Authors' handwriting may be almost illegible. The manuscript may be full of alterations, crossings-out and interlineations (that is, writing squeezed in between the lines). If the author is not near enough to consult easily, you might be faced with awkward decisions. Should you type what you think is intended, or should you wait until you can get confirmation from the author? By choosing the latter course, you may find yourself held up for a long time. Bad handwriting, and even bad and much-corrected typescripts, can seriously delay your progress, which inevitably reduces your earning power.

Despite these drawbacks typing has a great advantage over many other kinds of self-employment: you can work at home for a client anywhere in the country. This is the sort of work which young people living in deprived areas should strive for. They are very unlikely to find much house-cleaning or lawn-mowing work in the council estates where they live, and should seek the opportunities for work outside their home areas.

Finding Information and Work

If you go into the reference section of a public library you will find a number of journals and magazines on display. Pick out ones such as the *New Statesman*, the *Spectator*, *The Times Higher Educational Supplement*, the *Tablet*, and the *Church of England Newspaper*. They all contain a number of 'small ads', and among these you will find some offering typing services. These will give you an idea of the rates which are currently being charged – usually they are quoted as so much per 1000 words. In addition a charge is made for each carbon copy, and the total paid for these can often exceed the actual typing charge. With photocopying tending to replace carbons now, you may have to take your top copies to the nearest photocopier if a number of copies are required, and this can be expensive and unprofitable. If, however, you can establish good connections for regular work, you should aim at buying your own photocopier eventually.

To obtain typing work you should insert a small ad in the appropriate journals. You should look around for smaller and less expensive papers in which to advertise. Often the student bodies at universities and polytechnics have their own modest publications. You should try and find out what they are and who edits them by writing to the secretary of the appropriate students' union. The addresses of the universities etc may be found in *Whitaker's Almanack* and several other reference books, especially those dealing with higher education. A browse through the pages of *The Writers' and Artists' Yearbook* might suggest other suitable publications in which to advertise.

What Services Might You Provide?

If you are a competent typist you might consider offering a duplicating service as well. (You would, of course, need more equipment, and more space in which to work, store paper and envelopes etc.) There are many organisations which have occasional need for such a service. Even those which produce publications such as news-sheets and small magazines find it more convenient to give the work out than do it themselves; a small magazine involves a lot of typing, and decisions on how it should be set out. Duplicated magazines can be made most attractive. Gestetner have produced model magazines to show how this can be done, and it is worth while finding out as much about this as possible, and discovering what aids are available.

Apart from the work of typing, the collation and assembly of pages is time-consuming. You therefore need to agree a special rate with your customer before undertaking this sort of work. But you should remember you might be able to enlist the help of your family and friends in folding pages and stapling them.

Sometimes a customer wishes you to undertake the job of distribution, and supplies you with a list of subscribers. Although this can be an extra source of income, it can also give you serious headaches. You may have to cope with changes of address, new subscribers and the deletion of old ones, and so on. It is best to demand a new list for every distribution and to avoid the responsibility for amending one progressively. Writing and filling envelopes and affixing stamps can be tedious, too. But again your family and friends might help.

Car Washing

This may sound like the sort of job done by boy scouts on a Saturday, but there are people who make a business of cleaning cars. They often have contracts with motor dealers to clean all the cars in their showrooms and on their forecourts. The vehicles on display need to look really smart and gleaming, and if they are standing in the open for long they can get very dusty, spattered with bird-droppings, or stained with dead leaves. An old car just taken in part-exchange can need extensive cleaning and polishing to make it look attractive for a customer.

This work can also include looking after the interiors of cars, sponging the leather upholstery and putting a vacuum cleaner over the carpets. If you are looking after a collection of caravans and trailers, you will certainly be required to give them a thorough cleaning both inside and out.

Modelmaking

Young people often have considerable skill as modelmakers. They have acquired it making aircraft, arranging soldiers in battle scenes, and creating villages. The range of demand for modelmaking is wide: some models can be sold as toys, others as collectors' items. Carefully painted model soldiers attract the attention of both young and old people. If you have the skill to cast your own figures, so much the better, but it is possible to buy unpainted figures which you can then paint in accurate colours.

Children and collectors are not the only people interested in models, and although the market for toy models should not be minimised, you should be aware of other openings. If you take a walk through a large shopping area – such as London's West End – you will see how widely models are used in display. Ignore the tailors' dummies and note all the other objects – usually they have been combined to follow a particular theme, such as a Christmas scene, Paris in the spring or a sun-bleached desert island for summer. In one short walk you might see such diverse objects as suede rhinos, pink elephants, mini rocking-horses, human shapes made out of stuffed sacking, birds in gilded cages, macaws in hoops, palm trees, Spanish galleons and Empire State buildings.

Somebody has to make all these models. If you are clever with your hands and have an ingenious imagination, it could be you. Arranging the displays is usually in the hands of the display designer or manager at the particular shop or store, but such executives do not as a rule carry out the actual work of constructing the models. These jobs are given out to people they know to be reliable. It is a matter of breaking into this group, and becoming known for what you can do, so that when a particular type of model is required, your name is mentioned. Obviously you have to get in touch with the display designers and convince them of your talent.

Modelling Figures

It has not been possible to find a school-leaver who has actually broken into this field, but the experiences of a family of East European refugees who came to Great Britain in the 1960s are relevant. The mother and daughter were both skilled needlewomen. The father, who was unable to work because of disability, was able to give them instruction in the composition of a plastic material from which they could mould dolls' faces. Undoubtedly, their initial success was largely due to the use of this material, plus the skill with which they formed pleasing baby faces.

They began by making a range of baby dolls, dressed very

finely. The mother took these as samples to the buyers at leading London stores. Fortunately, the buyer at one of the most prestigious stores was interested and placed a small order. This led to others, and they could easily have settled into a routine of making the same type of doll over and over again. Instead, they began to experiment with historical figures. They dressed some dolls in national costumes, and others as schoolgirls, girl guides, ballerinas, and so on.

It was now a short step to entering the field of display because they already had connections with the stores. They began to move away from human dolls and made models of animals, both realistically and in a comic caricature form. Once their imaginations were let loose by producing pandas, snakes and camels with various human characteristics to amuse the window-gazers, they were able to think up fantastic space creatures and then to construct weird settings for them. A display theme for Christmas could keep them busy for weeks. Unfortunately, ill-health made them cut down and eventually cease their work, but their example (and they had to make their way in a strange country where they could not speak the language very well) is worth noting and trying to follow.

Other Areas

Another branch of modelling is the construction of small sets. These are used extensively by architects, who will commission modelmakers to build a very small-scale, accurate replica of an area which is to be redeveloped, or a building which is to be erected.

You might also consider museum work. Walk round a museum and observe the many model displays illustrating information for the public – for example, how the mountains were formed, what London was like under the Romans, and how a coal-mine is ventilated.

Think of the Possibilities

It would not be right to pretend that a school-leaver could at once begin working on his or her own account making models of this sort. They are cited as examples of work available to people who have made a name for themselves in these fields. It is encouraging to know, however, that modelmaking has extensive possibilities, and these examples might provide ideas for work well within your range which could provide opportunities.

Doll Repairing

Allied to modelmaking is dollmaking and therefore doll repairing and restoring. At one time there were lots of 'dolls' hospitals' scattered about, but their number now seems to be fewer. This might mean there are more opportunities to become a doll repairer. It is an interesting form of work, and can range from simple repairs of favourite dollies to difficult painstaking restoration of historic dolls worth hundreds of pounds.

Bicycle Repairing

For the mechanically minded who have limited resources both in premises space and equipment, bicycle repairing can be a good opening. The work need not be confined to bicycles either. Other forms of transport, such as prams, push-chairs and shopping-trolleys, occasionally need repairs. Apart from garages and dealers' shops there are often few places where such repairs can be undertaken.

If you would like information about this work, two books can be recommended: *Bicycles, how to ride and maintain them*, by Diana Gribble and Hilary McPhee (Kestrel), and *The Penguin Book of the Bicycle*.

China Repairing

Like doll repairing, this is work which can range from mending comparatively cheap pieces of crockery to restoring priceless artefacts to their original glory. (The classic example of china repairing was the piecing together of the Portland Vase.) There is always work to be done, but you might find it difficult to get sufficient to make it a full-time business. It could, however, be linked with some similar occupation or part-time employment. This is a field in which instruction is necessary and classes are available in London at Robin Hood's Workshops, 18 Bourne Street, Sloane Square, London SW1. If you live outside London you should enquire of your local education authority whether there are any classes in your district.

Chapter 4

Some Personal Experiences

The aim of this chapter is not just to show what certain people have achieved at 16, but to provide real-life illustrations of how much can be within your reach even without enormous reserves of experience or money. The main points to arise from the following examples are that you should recognise your skills as being the possible basis for successful self-employment and then remain alert to what might be demanded and where there might be a market for your work; your business can then be adapted and expanded accordingly. Given initiative and a sense of adventure, anything is possible.

THEATRICAL COSTUMIER

June had no intention of founding her own business. In fact, she is not yet certain whether she can claim to have done so successfully; so far she has made very little profit, perhaps no profit at all if she were to take all her outlay into consideration. If it hadn't been for her mother's support and encouragement she would have abandoned the idea months ago. Yet she has made a lot of progress, and her business is gaining momentum. One thing is leading to another, and personal recommendations are bringing her more and more customers. She has every reason to expect that in another year her little business will be on a firm footing.

For many years now June's mother has been closely associated with a local dramatic society, not as a performer but as its wardrobe mistress. Because the society had no permanent premises of its own, she began to store costumes in her attic. Gradually she accumulated what seemed to her a sizeable collection. Other societies found out what she had available, and when they needed items they would ring her up. From time to time, other groups or individuals would make enquiries. If she lent anything, June's mother would make a small charge which she passed on to the dramatic society to help their finances.

When June left school she tried hard to get a job, fully expecting she would find work in the local engineering firm where her father had been employed. But there were no jobs there, and none suitable anywhere else.

Without any intention of doing more than lending an occasional hand, June began to help her mother to sort out the miscellaneous items in the attic. Some had hardly been looked at for years, because no one had put on a play where these pieces of costume were required. There were old hats with battered feathers; a lot of ancient shawls pushed down in a tea-chest and getting a little damp; odd waistcoats; stiff-winged collars; a clergyman's surplice; maids' lace aprons; and various faded dresses, long out of fashion.

Almost everything wanted washing. Many wanted repairing. Taking some trouble, June and her mother greatly improved almost the entire stock, ironing items, airing them, and hanging them up on coat-hangers from lines rigged across the attic.

June is handy with her needle and her mother's sewing machine. She gave some of the old dresses an entirely new look by altering the bodices and stitching on new lace, beads or spangles. Modern dresses were made to look like Victorian ones, and even some of the men's modern jackets were converted into tailcoats and given velvet collars.

Getting the Business Started

It was while she was doing these various jobs that June began to wonder whether there were not the makings of a business here. She had heard of a friend who had borrowed a costume from a professional repository, and been charged £7 for having the costume for one day only. Nor had she regarded this charge as excessive – a costume which required numerous accessories, such as a hat, shawl, reticule and shoes, could well cost more.

June realised she would have difficulty finding sufficient customers to earn enough money to live on. To begin with, only those people who had used the collection in the past would know about it, and they had been used to paying only a nominal sum for their borrowings. If they were asked to pay an economic sum would they continue to borrow at all? But then, thought June, there must be a much wider demand. Other people manage to make a livelihood by hiring out clothes, so why shouldn't I?

First, however, the question of who actually owned the costumes had to be decided. The collection had been begun by the dramatic society, nobody quite knew when, but June's mother had added to it greatly at her own expense. She had made many of the garments herself. Others had been made by the actors, and others still had been acquired for particular productions. June's mother had also got into the habit of buying odd items at second-hand sales, merely because she felt they would come in handy some time.

June's mother raised the question of ownership at the next meeting of the society's committee. The members there were not greatly concerned, as long as the society would be able to get costumes at a reasonable charge. So they happily agreed to recognise her mother's ownership of the collection. In return, June's mother made a donation of £10 to the society's funds.

With this decided, she handed over the entire collection to her daughter and June began to look around for clients. She had to explain tactfully to those people who had customarily come to the collection for assistance, that she was now running it as a business. She would give them preferential terms as old customers, but they would be charged rather more than in the past.

Early Disappointments

June's first adverts appeared in shop windows around the town. Eventually a man telephoned. He was organising a Saturday fair. 'What I need are some sort of Disneyland fantasy suits. I saw some people dressed as rabbits last year at Tunbridge Wells. They came into the pub where I was sitting, and the sight of a green and pink rabbit leaning on the bar made quite a sensation – especially when they took their heads off to drink their beer. I don't suppose you've any suits like that?' Sorrowfully, June had to admit that she hadn't.

She had other disappointments. Several people who came to look at her costumes were very uncomplimentary. They poked about at them and didn't find anything they wanted. She lacked variety. Although she had a number of crinolines and dresses with bustles, as well as several men's frock and tailcoats, she had no great range even in these Victorian clothes. Neither did she have anything of an earlier period except a greasy three-cornered hat, but still several demands were for mediaeval costumes – doublets and hose (very popular for Shakespeare plays), short cloaks, men-at-arms' chain mail, conical head-dresses for Plantagenet ladies, and garments of that sort. June couldn't even kit out the actors for a Bible play, when all they needed was later supplied by tea-towels and blankets. What was more disappointing was that several people who found the sort of costume they required, discovered that June's selection would not fit them. All in all, these early experiences were very disheartening.

Turning Fortunes Around

As June couldn't provide what the majority of people wanted, her mother cautioned her to go easy on advertising. She thought that until the collection was expanded to a much larger range, it would be wrong to encourage callers. The collection would get a bad name which might be difficult to live down, and the notices were therefore taken out of the shop windows. Although June continued to provide costumes to people who knew her, she used this period to build up her stock.

The collection was built up from numerous sources – friends, jumble sales, and the school drama club which had six beefeaters' costumes complete with spears left over from their production of Fielding's *Tom Thumb*. Ex-servicemen bequeathed her sets of battledress. The flea market provided some German helmets, a Nazi tunic and an American GI's suit of olive-drab. She was given Chinese parasols, a big feather fan, bridesmaids' dresses, old silver shoes, walking sticks, a child's Red Indian outfit, and a tutu ballet-skirt.

She made other items herself. Friends who became interested in her venture were most helpful. Under one lady's direction she converted her old red winter coat into a guardsman's tunic, complete with epaulettes and sergeant's stripes. The skirt of the coat was trimmed with old fur and made into a costume suitable for a Russian dancer. Every old garment which came into the house was carefully examined and its possible alteration and use discussed.

June also realised she needed more than costumes. She

bought a set of beards and moustaches, with gum arabic to fix them. Advertisements by other theatrical costumiers indicated the need for wigs. She got in touch with a wholesale dealer and bought a number of wigs, a box of grease-paints, comic masks, flags, bunting, and a supply of streamers and cardboard trumpets. Before she was ready to advertise again, June had spent a considerable sum of money. The collection had grown too big for the attic and much of it now had to be housed in a large garden shed.

Despite this outlay of capital and effort, business was very slow at coming in. She obviously had to overcome the bad impression her earlier start had created. Yet at Christmas time she did very well. She provided quite a number of costumes for an amateur pantomime, and the hiring fees for these (although the organisers were reluctant to pay because their show was for charity) amounted to a nice little sum.

She also loaned crinolines and Victorian dress to be worn by the staff of a local store which was celebrating its centenary. There were, in addition, one or two demands for fancy-dress parties. If she had had a Santa Claus outfit she could have loaned it out several times, but it had never occurred to her to get one. Despite this, her takings over the Christmas period were very encouraging. She realised, however, that this time of year was exceptional and she could not expect the same level of demand to be maintained throughout the year.

After this, June began to cast her publicity net wider and to discover useful allies. She got to know a family which not only ran a stable but had a number of old carriages for hire. These were often loaned out to take part in some parade or historical pageant. The people using them sometimes wanted to dress up, and if they made enquiries about this, the stable manager would recommend June.

At much the same time she became acquainted with the proprietress of a local hall used for receptions, dances etc. This lady displayed a poster June had devised, and through her June received several enquiries about fancy dress.

The Current State of the Business

June admits she is not yet firmly established. Business is beginning to come along steadily, and people calling at her home often find several others there sorting out possible costumes. When a group of people are concerned in some venture such as a play or party, June's receipts can be considerable. But she still wants to add to her collection, and some items have to be bought, although she gets a lot from her friends. Her immediate neighbours never throw anything away without first consulting her to see whether she could make use of it. Nor do they go on holiday without bringing back some things which enhance her collection.

Because she began in a haphazard way, June did not keep proper accounts until fairly recently. So she does not have an accurate record of what she has spent or received. She knows she must be out of pocket, but she possesses a great deal of stock to show for it.

Her most recent advance is an entry in the Yellow Pages which she regards with pride. Although she has now had her eighteenth birthday, she feels justified in saying that at 16 she was her own boss.

COMPUTER PROGRAMMER

Jeremy's ambition was to be a rock star. He was interested, too, in electronics, which is not surprising as the two are closely allied. But electronics was only a hobby – Jeremy had no idea of making it a career.

When he was 14 Jeremy bought a computer kit and assembled it. His interest in computers took off. He discovered he had abilities with computers which far exceeded his friends' talents. He realised he was a 'natural' computer programmer when, after a little while, people began to come to him for advice.

He was 16 when he wrote a book on computers. Now, at 18, he has four more in print. There is a great demand for informed articles on computers as anyone can see by looking at the row of specialised computer magazines offered for sale in newsagents. Jeremy has cashed in on this demand and now earns a good income as a freelance writer.

He has needed very little capital to establish himself. His computer and word processor are his main items of equipment. His office is a small attic in his parents' house. There he works surrounded by books and papers. Success has come to him so suddenly and unexpectedly that he can still hardly believe it. His advice to other teenagers is to make sure they realise what their talents might be and to make full use of them.

CATERER

There are problems in setting up as a caterer. The local health authority has to be satisfied that your kitchen is up to standard and hygienic. There is more about this in Chapter 5. There is also a great failure rate of cafés and restaurants.

However, *Sue* and *Marylin* decided that they lived in a promising locality for a sandwich bar, despite there already being places where sandwiches and rolls were sold. They also realised that the local bakery had a special sandwich counter which was set out and manned every morning for early customers. But the two girls argued that this was not very convenient for many working people.

Judging a Location's Potential

They saw that in recent years there had been developments which altered the shape of the locality. A big new office block had been built, and several small factories had opened near it. The shopping area was some distance from these work-places, and unless people actually came through the shopping area, they found the bakery out of their way.

Sue's parents live in a terrace house. Not so long ago there were fields and woods behind it. Now the land is occupied by the office block and the one-storey factories. There is a large car park immediately behind their garden.

The house has no front garden at all. Its small bay window opens directly on to the pavement. Sue's father made enquiries about whether anyone would object to a business being started there. As the next house was already a jobbing builder's, the planning authority raised no objection to his proposal to convert the front room into a shop. The window was also altered to let the girls serve customers as they passed.

The situation, as they expected, was ideal. Once the word got about that sandwiches were being sold here, Sue and Marylin were never idle. They were exceptionally busy from early in the morning until about 9 am. Things then slackened off because the majority of customers were at work. Business became very brisk again during the lunch period and slackened off in the afternoon.

Judging Demand

The girls had some difficulty at first judging how much bread and fillings they would require. They ran short of some foods and had too much of others. They also tended to get in one another's way, but soon learned how to work together efficiently by concentrating on different jobs. During the rush periods they would work quickly side by side at the counter.

Almost from the start there was a demand for many other refreshments besides sandwiches, such as apples, oranges, bananas, crisps, chocolate and soft drinks. They had to expand their stock and buy a refrigerator to keep food in, and were also persuaded to get an ice-cream refrigerator installed. This cost them nothing as it was put in by the ice-cream supplier, but it is a matter of some difference of opinion. Sue thinks it attracts custom. Marylin believes it takes up valuable space which the ice-cream sales don't justify.

Publicity

The girls recently had a board erected above their window. It reads: SUE'S SANDWICH SHOP. Of course, it is really a joint business. The girls pay Sue's father a rent, and share the profits. The board, with each word beginning with a large 'S', is effective publicity and merely underlines the fact that the business is now on a firm footing. The girls are, in fact, now thinking of expansion.

Problems for the Future

'If only we could have a sales point at the bottom of the garden,' Sue has suggested, 'and could sell to people in the car park!' But there are problems which would have to be overcome, such as gaining planning permission.

They also have a worry. So far all the businesses, both in the office block and the factories, are small. If a larger business should move in – perhaps taking over most of the floors in the office block, or several of the factory units – it might well set up its own canteen and even throw it open to neighbouring firms. This could be serious competition for Sue's Sandwich Shop, which relies on the fact that there are no other caterers apart from the bakery and a public house half a mile away. They will have to rise to the challenge by keeping a close eye on quality and value.

ESTATE AGENT

John was not an estate agent at the age of 16, but he was heading in the direction of owning his own business; he had been working on his own account even while he was at school. For John has always been 'business-minded' and on the look-out for ways to make money. He began delivering newspapers when he was 13 – the fact that he had to get up very early in the morning never deterred him. Before long he had been able to buy himself an expensive bicycle and had a nice balance in his National Savings account. It became apparent to everyone – parents, friends and teachers – that John was a born entrepreneur.

When this word appeared on one of John's school reports, his parents wondered how his teacher had come to this conclusion. Apart from John's newspaper round, there was nothing they could think of which his school would know about him in this respect. It then came out that John had set up a thriving little business within the school. He had begun by suggesting to his teachers that he clean their cars in the lunch break. Soon he had regular commissions from them. He then put forward a further proposition: he would serve tea and biscuits in the staff room.

This was something revolutionary, because the staff room was regarded as prohibited territory for a pupil. But John pointed out that other ranks in the army served meals in the officers' mess. Perhaps this comparison swung the headmaster over, and he gave his consent for an experiment. After all, the current arrangements were far from ideal, and John's reputation as a reliable worker had been established through his car-cleaning.

John was as good and better than his word. After a few weeks he had startled the teachers by appearing with a black bow in place of his school tie. A little later he replaced his blazer with a black jacket with satin reveres. He did his best to act the perfect waiter, much to the staff's amusement and admiration. Apart from one or two little accidents he succeeded perfectly and the teachers liked him. He never took advantage of his privileged position by being forward or impertinent, so they were all genuinely sorry when the time came for him to leave school.

The Move into Property

It was this sense of adventure which stood John in good stead when he met a young man in the same mould who had just returned from Canada after becoming involved in property dealing. He had bought a large old house, repaired and decorated it, and then let it to students. After a while he had sold it for a profit and started buying more property.

Hearing these experiences, John decided he could do similar things. He volunteered to help his new friend in the work of renovating the most recent property he had bought, and his last school holidays were spent painting and papering. His friend, although self-taught, had become quite expert at renovations. John was able to pick up all sorts of practical hints from him.

Determined to be self-employed, the main venture John decided on after leaving school was estate agency. He had learned from his friend's experiences that anyone could set up as an estate agent. There are, of course, qualifications for estate agents and most belong to a professional body such as the Incorporated Society of Valuers and Auctioneers, or the Royal Institution of Chartered Surveyors. However, John decided he would get himself established first, and obtain the qualifications later. He realised that, being unqualified, his scope would be greatly restricted, but he merely intended at first to find buyers for his friend's properties.

The business began when his friend purchased a tiny little shop and placed it at John's disposal. They installed a telephone and erected a sign saying PORTLAND PROPERTIES. The business was very much a partnership. John's friend owned the shop, signed the forms for the telephone, and acted on behalf of Portland Properties whenever an older person was needed. But John sat in the shop, answered the telephone, talked to enquirers, handed out keys for people to inspect property, and so on.

Progress

John has now taken over the business entirely. In the five years since leaving school he has learnt a lot about agency work. He has acquired bigger premises in a busier part of town. This enables him to employ a small staff which includes a young newly qualified surveyor, a typist, and an older lady who works part time taking people by car to view houses for sale.

KNITTER

Ann has always been an excellent knitter. Her mother taught her at an early age, and the standard of their work is well above the average.

Ann's mother has sold knitted garments for many years, and a year or two ago she bought a knitting machine to help her produce articles more quickly. So when Ann left school the foundations of a business were already laid.

However, Ann has an accomplishment which her mother does not possess. Being inventive and artistic she is able to devise her own patterns, and the resultant garments are often very eye-catching. She has put on displays which have attracted considerable attention and resulted in important orders.

Ann has also become associated with a local society which spins and dyes wool. The ladies in this society are not really concerned with making money. They buy raw fleeces from local farms, comb and wash the wool, and then spin it. They each have their own old-fashioned spinning wheel and they meet to spin in company – half a dozen wheels whirling in unison.

Ann only occasionally uses the wool spun by these ladies, but by being involved with the society she has made many contacts. She says, 'You need to know people who are interested in wool and knitting. If you are good, they will talk about you, and customers will come to you. For instance, many people are fascinated by the sight of ladies spinning wool in the old way – for they often appear at craft fairs. If they would like something made from it, they are shown examples, some of which are my handiwork knitted to my own patterns. I get many orders in this way. I never seem to be short of work.

Sometimes, in fact, I have more than I can cope with, and my mother has to come to the rescue.'

STAMP DEALER

Ian has been a dealer since he began collecting stamps at the age of 10. Advertisements in boys' comics attracted his attention. He wondered how dealers could give away such attractive free stamps to anyone who asked for 'approvals'. After a little thought he concluded there must be a lot of money to be made from this business.

When he first offered a selection of stamps for his schoolmates to inspect, they were not very impressed. He had mounted a lot of stamps which were surplus to his collection and his friends were contemptuous; they could have prepared as good or better sheets themselves. Ian realised they were only likely to buy stamps they did not possess, so this meant he had to get hold of some unusual ones.

Developing a Business Brain

Ian then made a bold decision. He chose not to continue as a stamp collector, but to become a dealer instead. So he took some of the best stamps out of his album – the very ones he took the greatest delight in – and placed them on sale, pricing them from the latest catalogue. His friends regarded these stamps with envy, and before long Ian began to sell them.

Fortunately he also found someone to advise him – his sister's boyfriend who was also a philatelist (collector and student of postage stamps). He was rather worried when he discovered that Ian was selling off his collection, and wanted to know what he was charging. It amused him to learn that Ian had been asking and getting considerably more than the stamps were really worth. He was surprised that his school-fellows had never realised they could have bought similar ones much cheaper at a big dealer's. Ian was a little upset at hearing this. He had merely asked the price set out in the catalogue, although he had to confess that he had used some of his takings to buy further stock from a dealer in the city and had sold these stamps at a profit. But wasn't this, after all, what business was all about?

Ian's adviser felt that he would run into trouble from his

friends if he continued on this course and suggested another approach. It so happened that he worked in the head office of a well-known bank and his department received a large amount of overseas mail. He thus came into possession of a large number of foreign stamps. He himself was a specialist collector but only retained those which were of special interest to him. The rest he passed on to Ian.

Ian was soon inundated with stamps. The great majority were duplicates. He had hundreds of the same value stamps from France, the USA, Holland and Germany. But among them he got occasional ones from exotic parts of the world, such as Samoa, Kuwait, the Maldives.

Word of his enterprise spread round his family and friends. Large envelopes of stamps came to him almost every week. He sold the interesting specimens to his schoolmates at prices suggested by his sister's boyfriend, and with the others he made up packets of 20 and 50 for sale to new collectors. He tried to make these packets interesting, like lucky dips, with a few unusual stamps in each. This tempted even some of the more experienced collectors at school, and provided them with specimens to swop. Ian also kept all the British stamps which came his way and made them up in packages for dealers. For these he received small sums.

Forming Connections

Ian's interest brought him into contact with other dealers, even while he was at school. His father arranged for him to see a philatelist who was a fellow member of his golf club. This man had a couple of rooms in his house entirely devoted to stamps. He conducted a large correspondence with collectors and dealers throughout the world. He thought Ian could be of assistance to him, by putting him in touch with the world of schoolboy collectors with whom he had had no contact.

So Ian became a sort of agent for this man, getting stamps for him, and selling his stamps to schoolfellows, neighbouring collectors, and even to people in other towns. By the time he left school he had a lot of valuable connections.

His father's friend then decided to retire from dealing in stamps and to devote himself to collecting, mounting exhibitions, and writing about stamps. He handed over the whole of his stamp-dealing business to Ian, who was able to continue being his own boss.

STREET THEATRE

Tom and *Susan* are Americans whose home is in Long Beach, California. They work both in California and in neighbouring states. For the last two years they have come to Great Britain during the summer, and have found sufficient work to pay for their flight, food and lodging.

Both Tom and Susan are now over 20, but Tom has been working in street theatre since he was 14, and Susan has been in the business since she met Tom three or four years ago. They are very extrovert and confident. Tom comes from a family with theatrical traditions, but Susan's background is entirely different.

Some people have referred to Tom and Susan as 'buskers', but they have never gone in for entertaining theatre queues, nor for performing in the corridors of the London Underground. Their act needs an audience to stand and watch them, so they put it on in places such as Covent Garden, and at fairs and festivals. If they can find a place where chairs are available, or with a grassy slope where the audience can sit, so much the better.

The Nature of the Show

They were to be seen in June 1985 at the Rochester Dickens Festival. They took part in the procession through the town which marked the opening of the festival. With their bizarre costumes and painted faces they attracted a lot of attention. They call themselves the Victorian Circus Theatre, and in the procession, as they waved their Stars and Stripes banner, they caught the style of the traditional American circus entering a town.

Tom and Susan are well organised. They have headed notepaper bearing the title and address of the Victorian Circus Theatre. The paper also carries a picture of a ballerina riding a circus horse, although this is a fiction in the sense that their circus has no animals, no acrobats, nothing but the simplest of props. When they need help they may enlist one or two boys and girls. These assistants, suitably draped and fitted with a horse's head, form the only animal to appear in their acts, if one excludes a puppet giraffe.

In the main, however, Tom and Susan rely on mime and a few simple changes of costume. Tom assumes a large red nose to play the clown, a huge black moustache when he's the villain, a cloak and top hat when he's a magician, and when he's a weight-lifter he takes off his coat and rolls up his sleeves.

Susan wears a long white lacy dress trimmed with green ribbons, a coloured sash and a straw bonnet. Her costume does not permit much versatility, but she can become a mysterious figure by wrapping herself in a black cloak, or turn into a ghost by putting a white sheet over her head.

With no scenery changes to hold proceedings up, and these simple rearrangements of costume, Tom and Susan's act goes ahead at a lively pace. The volunteer helpers hold out the tightrope (along the ground) and Susan balances herself precariously on it, one hand holding a small parasol, the other extended. Then Tom lifts tremendous (imaginary) weights, his legs trembling, his eyes expressing the immense strain he is under and the doubt as to whether he'll succeed. Much of the effect of every act is gained by their facial expressions and particularly by the way both Tom and Susan use their eyes.

They also sing – not too musically – and pretend to conjure. In fact, Tom gives hints of being a better conjurer than he appears to be. He is also a juggler, and has some skill with three coloured handkerchiefs.

Apart perhaps from this little bit of juggling, their entire act could be done without any specialised training (although, as it happens, they have both had some training). Basically, they have developed this act themselves. It is all make-believe, but well-done make-believe. They have the gift of persuading their audiences to enter with them into a fantasy world, and this may be their greatest skill.

Organisation

Tom and Susan began the Victorian Circus Theatre shortly after they first met. Gradually they have made it known both in America and Great Britain. They go to considerable trouble to find out the sort of events at which their act might be welcome. They have established connections with the organisers of fairs and festivals, and even when they cannot be included in the official programme they can sometimes obtain permission to put on a show somewhere at the side. They then pass round a hat, and the takings can be quite substantial over a couple of days.

They take care over the planning of their tours so that they can make the fullest possible use of their time and cut their travelling to a minimum. They choose to stay at places from which they can fulfil several engagements in the vicinity. Making such arrangements from California is not easy, but British teenagers wishing to arrange a similar tour in this country would not find it half so difficult.

Tom wrote in February 1985: 'Susan and I spent Christmas and the New Year holiday performing on a cruise ship in the Caribbean. I wrote a Readers' Theatre version of *A Christmas Carol* and performed it on Christmas Day with 12 children aged 8 to 14 doing the other parts. We are making plans to be in England again next June. I'm now in the midst of a jumble of theatre scripts, maps, and British travel books, attempting to find places for us to stay during our travels.'

SOFT-TOY MAKERS AND DOLL DRESSERS

Jane had made 'cuddly' toys as a hobby for several years before she left school. At first she gave them all to the church's annual sale of work where they were displayed along with numerous other knitted teddy bears, felt mice, and clothes-peg dolls.

However, Jane was not satisfied with her own articles as they looked 'amateurish'. But when she compared them with the goods offered for sale in the leading stores, she realised that it only required a little more effort and care to bring her toys up to a professional standard.

The next time she had products on display at the sale of work they were clearly better than the other articles. She was pleased when people enquired who had made them, and even more pleased when one lady asked her to make one especially for her.

This set Jane off as a soft-toy maker. She did not think it would ever develop into a business. She got very few orders and never went in search of them. But when she left school and found no one to employ her, the idea of doing something on her own began to take shape in her mind.

Having a lot of time on her hands, she set about making a range of soft toys. When she had sufficient stock to form a display she applied for a position at the local craft fair. This took place on a Saturday afternoon, and she sat behind her little table from 2 to 5.30 pm while people milled around, staring at her goods, picking them up occasionally, and usually putting them down again. However, she sold one or two and decided to display her wares at similar events in the neighbourhood. Sales were slow and not especially encouraging, but among the sales she also received orders to make duplicates.

Jane's mother was enlisted to help. She first did so when Jane discovered that two fairs were being held on the same Saturday and needed someone to mind a stall for her. Her mother gradually became more involved, especially in the selling part of the business after they had come up with the idea of using retail outlets. She began to call on shops and was so good as a commercial traveller, despite a complete lack of experience, that Jane could not keep up with the orders obtained.

So Jane's father took over the sales side while her mother helped in the work-room. The schoolgirl hobby has now become a family concern.

Amanda has not been quite as successful as Jane, although she has progressed in a similar way. She does not make dolls; she dresses them. She too began doing this as a hobby, but on leaving school made a big effort to win orders.

At first she aimed only at 'old-fashioned ladies' in long gowns. Then she found that actual characters sold better. The basic doll could be given a moustache or beard which entirely altered its appearance and sex.

Her dolls are very expertly dressed. Amanda takes great pains, studying pictures of historical figures, so that Henry VIII really does look like Holbein's portrait and his doublet and hose are exactly right.

She also tried her hand at making dolls representing the Queen and Prince Philip, Mrs Thatcher, Winston Churchill, and other well-known figures. These were by no means as successful as the period characters, possibly because they were not good likenesses. Some customers would not have known that a doll represented Mrs Thatcher unless they had read the label, but few had much difficulty in recognising the one dressed as Queen Elizabeth the First.

Dressing these dolls, and especially those in a lot of finery, takes a considerable time, a lot of skill, and patience. They come expensive as a result and, because of their price, are not easily sold. Despite this, Amanda has sold enough to encourage her to continue. Her dolls are on display in a number of large stores, and orders come in steadily.

PORTRAIT ARTIST

Jim was told he could never support himself as an artist. People said his chances would be nil unless he went to an art school. His parents felt he ought to go either into a bank, the civil service, or something equally secure; he certainly had enough O levels to get into such jobs.

However, Jim stuck out against such a future. He wanted to be an artist and was determined to follow his ambition. 'After all,' he told his father, 'if I go into one of those jobs I'll be stuck there for life. And remember who's the artist recognised as the best in Britain at the moment – Francis Bacon. And did he go to art school? No! And he thanks heaven he never did.'

No one doubts Jim has talent. He can catch the likeness of a person in a few lines of crayon. He is equally good with a brush. He would certainly have done well at art shool, had he chosen to follow that path.

Eventually his father agreed to let him have his own way to an extent, coming to a gentleman's agreement to support Jim for at least a year. In that time, Jim would see how he managed as a professional artist. If it then became clear that he could never support himself in this way, he would give serious consideration to trying some other occupation before it was too late to begin a career.

The day after he left school, Jim set off to find customers in central London. He found fellow artists drawing portraits by Piccadilly Circus, at the base of Garrick's statue, and elsewhere. He joined them and spent several happy afternoons sketching away in the sunshine. Yet it was not the most satisfactory way of drawing portraits; he was up against a lot of competition and some of his rivals resented his intrusion. He had to work rapidly because sitters had other things to do besides having their likenesses sketched, and many of them, especially children, would not keep still. Once or twice a sitting had to be abandoned because of heavy rain, and while the fine weather brought crowds and business, it also brought the sightseers who would stand behind him and peer at every mark he made.

Adapting and Expanding the Business

So while it was still summer, Jim moved to the south coast. He took a haversack and a sleeping bag and slept out under a pier when the nights were warm. He did quite good business in the seaside resorts and eventually persuaded the manager of one of the larger hotels to allow him to set up a pitch in the corner of the foyer.

After setting up his easel and laying out his materials, Jim hung several of his sketches, oil paintings and landscapes on a screen. Although lots of people came in and out of the hotel, he had difficulty in getting anyone to pay serious attention to him. He therefore got a friend to pose while he painted her portrait. The sight of someone actually being painted soon drew idlers to stand around and watch.

It was not long before he had a commission. A lady wanted her teenage daughter's portrait. Jim took particular care over it, knowing that a pleasing likeness would probably bring another customer.

So it did. Although customers did not exactly queue to occupy the chair, he had enough to make his efforts successful. He also prevailed on those subjects who were not leaving the hotel immediately, to allow their pictures to be displayed until they did so. This was a good advertising ploy. Several people either brought friends to see their picture or pointed it out to other guests.

Jim found another outlet for his talents besides painting sitters. One day he was asked to copy a photograph. Then he made a large picture of a person who had been photographed in a group. A local resident, seeing what Jim had done, brought him an old sepia photograph to copy. It was so faded that Jim had difficulty making out the face and figure. But he did his best and the resultant portrait showed a healthy young man of about 28 with rich wavy fair hair. Jim asked his customer if it really resembled his friend. 'Oh, exactly,' came the reply, 'but it isn't a friend – that's me, 30 years ago.'

The summer season came to an end after the first fortnight in September. Work fell off, so Jim returned home. He had saved a very small sum, quite insufficient to see him through the winter, and he was keen to prove to his father that he could support himself.

Getting work as an artist in his home town was not at all easy. He painted some pictures of local scenes – the parish church, the entrance to the park, an old pump up a courtyard – and placed them for sale at the local artists' materials shop. No one seemed to want them. Then, one afternoon, Jim noticed a middle-aged couple looking at them through the window.

'Personally, I like them,' said the man.

'So do I,' agreed his wife. 'But at £45 each, they're a bit too much.'

The next day Jim affixed new price tags, making substantial reductions. Within the next fortnight, all the pictures were sold. Jim set about painting more.

Whether Jim could have supported himself throughout the winter solely by these efforts cannot be known. Before Christmas he had begun to help a photographer specialising in wedding photographs. Jim's other chief interest, photography, became a useful ally at this time and probably portraiture and photography jointly will eventually become his profession. Certainly he has at the moment no intention of becoming a bank clerk.

OTHER EXAMPLES OF SELF-EMPLOYMENT

Wholesaler. A television news-item carried the story of a schoolboy who has started a business as a wholesaler. He buys goods in bulk, storing them in his bedroom, and sells them to local grocers and general shops. He was shown delivering goods to a local shopkeeper.

Fashion designer. It was reported on the radio that a young girl had gone into business, designing and making fashion goods. She had found a ready market among young people of her own age, and had even interested buyers from the USA.

Wrought-iron craftsman. There was a recent television documentary shot in the Medway towns showing how they are suffering from the closure of the Chatham dockyard. It featured efforts being made in the area to create new jobs. Among these were one or two examples of people who had set up on their own account, including a young man (now aged 17) who makes various articles of wrought iron, such as gates, brackets, lamp-holders, and house-names. He set up a little while ago in vacant premises in the dockyard, where earlier craftsmen built HMS *Victory*.

Artificial-flower maker. A women's programme on television featured a girl who has established a good connection with retail stores. She makes artificial flowers out of felt, and others which are more realistic out of silk.

Carpet and textile designing. Two young designers from Leeds knew a lot about producing tufted rugs and soft furnishings but little about business.

To close this gap the girls visited Leeds City Council's department of Industry and Estates, Leeds Business Venture, the Small Firms Advice Centre and, finally attended a 'Be Your Own Boss' course in Halifax. This advice led to awards of £1500 from Leeds City Council, £2000 from the Royal Jubilee and Prince's Trusts and a balancing loan from the bank. MSC approved an Enterprise Allowance and production started in rented premises with basic equipment.

FREELANCE WORK

This chapter has concentrated on young people who have actually started their own businesses. But, as was pointed out earlier, being a freelance is much akin to having your own business.

The most common forms of freelance work, such as house-cleaning, baby-sitting, and gardening have already been described. Some talented young people are able to support themselves as freelance writers and artists, yet it must be acknowledged that your chances of being successful enough to rely on such work for a living are slim. However, many young people earn useful supplements to their incomes in this way.

A number of girls of 16 do, however, gain employment as freelance fashion models. Live models display clothes to fashion buyers and members of the public. Others are occasionally employed by a designer, who creates a garment by draping the material around the model, pinning pieces on, or cutting pieces away. Opportunities for photographic models are much more numerous, and this field is entirely occupied by freelances. Work is obtained through one of the model agencies. *Careers in Modelling*, published by Kogan Page, provides further information on this field.

FURTHER READING

The Careers and Occupational Information Centre (COIC) has published a book entitled *All Our Own Work* which includes a number of interesting articles about people who work for themselves. These cover dog grooming and clipping, gardening, sign-writing, running a record shop, the rag trade, child-minding, sandwich selling, and making clothes of netting. All these jobs are done by young people who have recently left school. The book also gives a lot of hints to those who wish to start their own business.

Chapter 5

Difficulties and Dangers

It is not at all easy being your own boss at 16. When you are 18 you are of age and free from various legal restrictions. You can also be free of one of the most irksome restrictions (as far as running your own business is concerned) when you become 17: you can have a licence to drive a car.

In law, until you come of age you are classed as a minor – or, as the law sometimes terms it, an infant. Before 1969, the age of majority was 21. This was lowered to 18 by the Family Law Reform Act 1969. In many respects it does not matter much whether you are of age or not. There are some areas, however, especially contracts, where special rules apply to minors.

CONTRACTUAL RESTRICTIONS

Here it might be appropriate to explain very briefly what is meant by contracts because they play an important part in all our lives, particularly for people in business.

A leading authority on the law (Anson) has defined a contract as 'a legally binding agreement made between two or more persons, by which rights are acquired by one or more to acts or forbearances on the part of the other or others.'

If you go into a shop you can acquire the right to goods by making a payment to the shopkeeper. The transaction is based on an implied contract. It was started by the shopkeeper making you an offer by placing his wares on sale at a certain price, and concluded by your acceptance of his offer and paying the agreed price. Lawyers divide this process into three parts: offer, acceptance and consideration.

You can see that whenever you buy something, whether it is a pair of shoes, a haircut or a train ride, you enter into a contract. Sometimes we make more formal contracts: there is an actual document, called a contract, which we and the other party have to sign. Contracts like this are necessary when we buy property or enter into a hire-purchase agreement. There are even more formal types of contract, made under seal, to which special rules apply. But we shall not bother with these. Let us confine ourselves to what are known as 'simple contracts'.

As contracts are such a part of our everyday life, it follows that even children are legally capable of being parties to them. However, the common law has always ensured that minors are protected from the possible results of their own inexperience and folly – at least, it has tried to do so.

One type of folly which the law envisaged was that minors would get themselves heavily into debt by ordering luxuries. The law has therefore tried to prevent this by making traders who deal with minors very careful about what they supply. Otherwise the trader may find that he will be unable to enforce payment when he presents the bill.

Until the passing of the Family Law Reform Act 1969, contracts by minors (except for 'necessaries' which will be explained later) were all voidable at the minor's option. In other words the minor could declare the contract void either before or after reaching 21, and the other party could not enforce it. The 1969 Act changed this to some extent. Contracts in which a minor acquires an interest of a permanent or continuous nature are valid and binding upon him until he disaffirms them. He must do this either during his minority or within a reasonable time after. (This applies to young women equally, of course.) Contracts to perform isolated acts, such as the purchase of goods which are not 'necessaries', are not binding unless the young party ratifies them within a reasonable time after majority. Contracts to repay money lent, or to be lent, to a minor are absolutely void.

Some contracts are, of course, greatly to a minor's advantage, such as a contract of apprenticeship (indentures); a minor may enforce such a contract, even though it cannot be enforced against him. A minor may also recover damages, but is not able to obtain 'specific performance', that is, an order from the court commanding the other party to carry out the requirements of the contract.

A contract for 'necessaries' has always bound a minor. 'Necessaries' have been defined as 'goods suitable to the condition in life of such infant and to his actual requirements at the time of the sale and delivery'. They are not to be confused with 'necessities' such as food, drink, clothing and shelter, which are essential to maintain life. Exactly what is a 'necessary' has to be decided in respect of each individual. What is a necessary for the son of a newspaper tycoon is probably not a necessary for the son of a shipyard worker.

After this diversion, you might ask what effect these legal rules have on young people trying to start in business on their own. The answer is that other business people are very wary about entering into a contract with a minor if there is any chance that the minor will disaffirm the contract. Nor will banks be willing to lend money.

RESTRICTIONS ON USING YOUR HOME

The majority of young people who start a business of their own base that business at their own home. It is the obvious place, for example, from which to run a typing service or to make rag dolls. But some words of warning are essential.

There may be legal restrictions on the use to which you can put the premises, even though the freehold belongs to you or your parents. There may be covenants on the property or requirements you have to meet.

Naturally, if the house or flat is rented, you must get your landlord's permission to run a business from it. If it belongs to your parents and they have given their consent to whatever you plan to do, you will have to find out whether there are any restrictive covenants on the property. These will be set out in the title deeds. There are covenants on many suburban properties which prohibit the owners from using the houses as business premises. It is, of course, unlikely that anyone would object to your using your home for typing manuscripts or addressing envelopes, but strictly speaking, if this is a business and conducting a business on the premises is in breach of the covenant, you should not do it. In practice, however, what is really prohibited is a business which is visible to everyone – such as a builder's yard or an estate agency with a display of 'Houses for Sale' in the window.

Avoid the Hazards

If you are changing the use to which your house is put – from a dwelling house, pure and simple, to a shop, office or workplace – you must tell the local authority's planning officer. You will find the address by looking up your local authority in the telephone directory. You may find that the change of use leads to a change in the rating of the house as well.

If you are intending to make structural alterations to the property you will need to have planning permission before you begin. You read in the previous chapter how Sue's father converted the front room of his house into a shop for selling sandwiches. He obtained planning permission to do so. If he had altered his bay window without official consent he might have been compelled to restore it to its original form.

If you are going to use premises for a business and other people will be coming there, either as customers or members of your staff, you will have to make sure that conditions are safe. You must also see that you are insured against accidents. If someone slips on your polished floor or trips over something you have left around, you will be held liable and may have to pay heavy compensation.

Your premises might be dangerous in a number of ways. They might contain dangerous machines, or have stores of dangerous materials. You might be working with something which gives off toxic fumes, or emits dangerous radiation. These extremes are unlikely, but it is surprising how many things can be dangerous either to those who handle them or to those who work in their vicinity. You must be safety conscious.

Fire, of course, is a hazard everywhere. It is especially likely in places where there are inflammable materials (now often marked as FLAMMABLE materials). Remember that the word 'inflammable' means that materials can burn very readily. It does not mean (as some people have thought) that they can't catch fire. Therefore, you must take care to see that the risk of fire on your premises is reduced to the minimum by installing fire extinguishers and clearly indicating the location of the fire exits. Passages and doorways must also be kept clear of obstructions. You should, of course, ask the local fire prevention officer to come and inspect your premises so that you can be sure you are doing everything necessary.

If you are preparing food on your premises, they must be clean and hygienic, along with your equipment. The public health officer will wish to inspect both of them, and you should get in touch with him before you start trading.

There are various officials who will be ready to give you help and advice on these matters – the local authority's planning and public health officers, the local fire service, and the Safety and Health at Work Executive. You will find their addresses in the telephone directory.

Play-Groups

Many young people think that because they are good with children they can start a play-group in their home. They would like to look after a number of small children whose parents are out at work all day. However, they need to be aware that planning permission is necessary for this, and that there is also a legal requirement to register the play group with the local authority. Young people of 16 are unlikely to obtain registration.

The alternatives are to take baby-sitting jobs or to obtain employment in a play-group, acting as an assistant under the direction of a supervisor. This would provide experience for opening a play-group when they are older.

LEGAL HAZARDS

Copyright

Some young people may think of playing music – they must realise there is a law of copyright. If they are to give public performances using music composed by someone else, there is a legal obligation to see that the composer is rewarded. This is done by paying a fee through the Performing Rights Society Ltd, 29 Berners Street, London W1A 4PP. They should enquire whether the hall in which they are booked is covered by a licence from the Society and if not, they must make other arrangements with it.

Disc jockeys playing records or cassettes often don't realise they are using copyright material. They need a licence not only from the Performing Rights Society but also from Phonographic Performance Ltd, 14–22 Ganton Street, London W1B 1LB.

Pyramid Selling

Inexperienced people are open to exploitation by unscrupulous operators. They may be persuaded to take part in schemes which have every appearance of being easy and honest ways of making money, but in fact are dishonest. Any money obtained through them is done so by fraud.

One such fraud is known as pyramid selling. You want to be able to recognise a pyramid selling scheme if it is proposed to you, so that you can give it a firm *no*.

Pyramid selling operates on the same principle as the 'chain letter'. The person who receives a chain letter is asked to send a sum of money (say £1) to the next person named on the letter. After doing this, he or she has to send out 10 similar letters to other people and add their names to the list. This (if they all respond) will bring in £10, a profit of £9.

It all seems innocent enough. But in order to persuade people to comply with the letters, the organisers include a veiled threat, such as a warning that 10 years' bad luck will descend upon anyone breaking the chain.

You may be able to recognise a chain letter at once, but it is not always so easy to spot a pyramid selling scheme, although it operates on the same principle of depending on people down the line for profits. You may be approached by someone who wants to sell you the right to supply some type of goods. You are asked to join his sales force and to assist in getting a number of your friends to act as sub-agents. You have to pay money to become an agent, and you receive similar amounts from the sub-agents you recruit. Although you may eventually get some goods to pass on, or to sell yourself, the main way you make money is through the recruitment of agents, not through the sale of goods.

Tricksters are inventive people and very persuasive. Some of their schemes are very well disguised; you can be greatly reassured when you see some of the high-quality goods you are being asked to assist in selling. But whenever you are approached with an idea of this sort, promising big rewards for doing very little, be cautious. Take legal advice if you are at all tempted and, unless you are completely satisfied that the scheme is an honest one – and never take the word of the person who proposes it to you – have nothing to do with it. Pyramid selling is prohibited by the Fair Trading Act 1973, so if you become involved you might find yourself in breach of the law.

Bookmaking

Some young people have been tempted to become bookmakers, often taking bets from people who assume they are passing them on to the betting shop. This is a very dangerous thing to do, not just because the law controls betting activities, but because you can lose large sums of money in this way – or be liable to pay large sums which you don't possess.

Leave bookmaking to the bookmakers. They have sufficient reserves to meet the occasional big wins, and if they realise they have laid themselves open to big losses should a particular horse win, they 'lay off' part of the risk by betting on the horse themselves.

Just imagine what an awkward position you would be in if you took a bet from a neighbour and the horse – an outsider at 100 to 1 – happened to win. Your neighbour would be jumping with excitement thinking he had won (say) £100. Then you would have to explain that you had never actually placed the bet with a betting shop but had 'stuck it' yourself. You might then have a liability beyond your means.

Chapter 6

Setting Up in Business

The examples given in Chapter 4 might have given you ideas about setting up in business yourself. You may therefore have read Chapter 2 again, and devoted some time to careful self-analysis. You have seen what you can do and what you can't and decided on a business where you feel there is a need. So you want to know how to begin? How do you actually set about it? Now is the time to apply the lessons of Chapter 4 to your own aspirations.

BUILDING ON EXPERIENCE

It might be useful to look a little more closely at some of the examples described in Chapter 4 and see how some of these young people started. Most of them continued with hobbies they already had while at school. It is true that June had not originated her collection of costumes – that was her mother's doing – but she had taken a keen interest in it, so her subsequent business was built on a foundation already laid.

John did not begin as an estate agent during his schooldays, but he had developed a business attitude which made it clear he was going to be his own boss in one field or another. Jane, Jeremy and Ian all developed their hobbies into businesses. Tom, Susan and Jim had all begun artistic careers, and merely continued them on leaving school.

It would seem that only Sue and Marylin deliberately set out to found a business without previous experience in that form of work. They were the most careful planners of all the cases which have been cited: they weighed up the needs of the district, the competition, and made a fair assessment of their chances of success.

Parental Help

Sue and Marylin were fortunate in getting the help and support of Sue's mother and father. Without them, and the use of the family home, they would not have been able to start. Parental help was invaluable also for June. Without her mother's initiative and her assistance in getting a clear title to the dramatic society's costumes, the business would never have got off the ground.

Ann also had a great deal of help and encouragement from her mother, and much of her training had been received at home. Jeremy's success is based on parental help with the provision of equipment and premises. Jim, too, was largely reliant on his parents. His father was very tolerant and understanding, but put a safety net under Jim's ambition by supporting him financially in return for a promise that he would look for a career if self-employment proved unsuccessful.

So perhaps the first thing to do, if at all possible, is to get the help of your parents. It is worth remembering that although being aged 16 is a hindrance in a number of ways, there are wonderful advantages.

The first is that you can obtain financial support from your family in the early critical period. The second is that in the family home you can have a base from which to operate. It is in many cases a well-equipped base, too, with a typewriter, a work-room, perhaps a lathe or a knitting-machine, a cooker and miscellaneous kitchen equipment. All these facilities are ready to hand for your use, free of charge.

The third advantage is that you may have an experienced person ready to train you. June, Jane and Ann were all trained by their mothers, but many young people are trained entirely by their fathers. Sometimes they don't even realise what they have picked up in the way of tricks of the trade, technical information and business connections. Many owe their father everything they know about such matters as handling carpenters' tools, adjusting car engines, looking after bees, grafting roses, and playing musical instruments.

Mothers and fathers often possess skills which they can lend to their children's early business undertakings. They can help with bookkeeping, provide transport, give legal advice, type letters, or design posters. Parents can also provide financial help by lending capital, but this is something which will be dealt with in the next chapter.

Work You Are Familiar With

It is best to decide to do something you are talented at or familiar with. Most of the examples in Chapter 4 were young people with a particular talent. June was a little different. She certainly had a talent for dressmaking and altering garments, but these skills did not direct her into becoming a theatrical costumier. She chose that business because she was familiar with it: she had seen her mother lending out costumes and knew what was entailed.

If you are familiar with a particular service – because you have often helped to serve in your uncle's shop, or have spent your summer holidays waiting on tables in a seaside boarding house – this is the sort of work you should aim at doing on your own account.

DEMAND FOR YOUR GOODS OR SERVICES

Take pains to discover, before you actually start, what the demand for your products or services is likely to be. Remember that demand has to be 'effective' demand. If you can only manage to produce your goods at a price higher than people are prepared to pay, you will have no effective demand at all. In other words, it is not enough that people should merely desire to have what you are offering.

It is often noticeable at craft fairs that many of the goods offered for sale, although they are delightful and most attractive, do not sell. They are priced much too high because their producers argue to themselves that this article is certainly 'worth' so much, and that article is 'worth' so much again. They use the idea of worth to price their goods and not the idea of effective demand.

Economic theory puts forward one or two ideas as to how prices are arrived at. The most persuasive is the law of supply and demand, where the price is determined when the two are in balance. Demand can be increased by reducing the price, and vice versa if articles are in short supply and demand for them is great; a rise in price will bring more of them on to the market and also reduce demand. So goes the theory, and no doubt for your purposes it is well to remember that you can increase effective demand by not asking too much.

You must see that you get a reasonable profit. But if your

goods can only be sold by reducing the price so low that it does not cover all the costs of production, including your own profit, then you should cease producing them.

Demand in Practice

Demand is not easy to assess. Some goods are always in demand, especially those, such as food, which are rapidly consumed. Bakers never find their market drying up, as bread and cakes continue to be in demand. However, people do not go on buying more and more garden rollers or Chubb's safes. Once they have bought one they will not need another for a very long time.

So you must weigh up what sort of demand there will be for the particular goods or services you propose to offer. Services are very similar to goods in patterns of demand. Neither ice-creams nor lawn-cutting are much in demand during the winter, and a householder will only need the house painting about once every four years. Even if you reduce the price on such services you will not induce a particular customer to increase his demand greatly, although you may win customers from other businesses.

Demand depends on a number of factors: location, season, fashion, weather, the state of employment in an area and the degree of competition. Sue and Marylin assessed the demand for their sandwiches very cleverly. They realised a market had been created by the arrival of the new factories, that it was not being satisfied by existing traders, and that it was in the area where Sue lived. Sue and Marylin realised they would have very little competition; the bakers' shops were in the wrong position for the new trade.

COMPETITION

It is no good starting a business where there is another already well-established unless it is clear that the rival cannot cope with all the existing demand, or – perhaps because a huge housing estate is being built nearby – with any growth in the market.

People starting up on their own should never try to compete with large established concerns or with big manufacturers. They cannot hope to match the big firms' expertise and efficient use of resources. It is wiser to go in for something which big concerns cannot do, for a speciality which requires individual skill or care.

This point was well made by the receptionist at a suburban hotel who was advising some visitors about the shopping facilities of the locality. 'If you wish to taste something special,' she told them, 'try some home-baked cinnamon bread. You won't find it in the supermarket or the big restaurant over the way, but go down to Martha's tea-shop – she serves it warm and thickly buttered. It's a treat. But you may have to wait until there's a free table.' It is by gaining a reputation such as this, and creating a demand which the big firms cannot meet, that a small business succeeds.

PARTNERSHIPS

You can be your own boss even if you are only jointly in charge. A partnership can be a useful way of supplying a business with all the skill and expertise it requires when you still have shortcomings in some areas. If you have the money and all the qualities needed you might as well carry on business alone, hiring any additional help you may require. If you have a partner, he or she will have to have a share in the profits and this will reduce your share.

However, even if you possess all the skill needed by the business, you may not have sufficient capital to get it started. You may then find that someone is willing to become a partner with you, not to contribute skill, but to provide the capital. Such a partner, who takes no active part in the running of the business, is known as a 'sleeping partner'. But having risked their money in a business, sleeping partners take a very keen interest in the business's finances and have a right to interfere if they see the active partners conducting affairs in ways likely to lead to loss.

Dangers

You should be very careful before you enter into a partnership or invite someone else to be a partner with you. If you are in business on your own, you are known as a 'sole trader'. This has the disadvantage that, if you are of age (and a 16-year-old is not) and your business goes bankrupt, you are personally liable for all its debts. In order to secure payment, your creditors can take all the assets of your business and, if necessary, all your personal property too.

The position is very similar if you are in a partnership. In this case you are jointly liable for the business's debts. If these have been run up through your partner's mismanagement it does not alter your joint liability, and all your personal property is at risk in the same way as if you were a sole trader. The choice of partner is therefore very important.

Advantages

Assuming, however, that your choice is a wise one, a partnership can be very successful and valuable. The number of partners need not be limited to one. While you are devoting yourself to that part of the business in which your skills and talents can be best employed, your partners can be covering branches of the work where you lack expertise or ability.

For example, while you are busy turning out concrete gnomes, a job for which you may be particularly well suited, one of your partners who is a car driver, and has, besides, a winning manner, is touring the country as a salesman. The third partner, the backroom boy, is looking after the clerical work, keeping the accounts, sending out invoices, and answering correspondence.

A partnership can be one way of getting yourself trained. This is very important for a young person. To start any business, however small and simple it might be, without adequate training is very difficult. It is one of the reasons why few school-leavers manage to do so. Even those with strong business instincts feel they cannot 'go it alone' right away. They either need a course of further education or, if they decide they can do without this, they look for a paid job where they can learn the essentials of the business they intend to set up. But if you can find a suitable business partner – perhaps someone who has already set up a business and needs help with it, or maybe your parents in an unofficial capacity – you may learn the ropes that way. You would, of course, need to have something you could offer on your side of the partnership.

START-UP FINANCE

Freelance

If you merely intend to be a freelance worker doing such jobs as baby-sitting, house- or office-cleaning, and gardening, you will need little or no capital.

A gardener may perhaps need a few tools, although most of these should be available at the place of work. More expensive equipment may be needed if work is taken on for a block of flats, a group of houses, or for a residents' association. It may be essential then to obtain a motor mower and your own spade, fork, clippers, secateurs etc.

In the majority of cases, freelance workers do not need to make elaborate estimates of income and expenditure or worry about cash flow problems. But you will have to work out how much you are likely to earn from your various activities and see whether this will be sufficient to keep you.

Remember that if you are working on your own account you have to pay a National Insurance contribution if you earn more than £34 a week (1985 figure). There is more about National Insurance in Chapter 7.

Business Finance and Accounting

If instead of working freelance, you intend to start an actual business, you must plan ahead much more carefully. Many businesses fail because important factors have not been fully considered in advance. In most instances, but not necessarily in all, a business requires premises, capital equipment and raw materials. If you are working from home you may not realise how much you are being subsidised by your parents. They may not be asking you for any money, but there is a cost – perhaps a number of costs – that they are bearing. You should really be paying for rent, rates, heating, lighting, and perhaps for telephone calls. You will not have a true idea of the profitability (or otherwise) of your business unless you take these subsidies into account.

You must also budget for expenditure on capital equipment, such as tools, machines and furniture. All items you need to carry on your business come under this heading – knitting machines, computers, lawn-mowers, typewriters, ladders, filing cabinets etc.

You will either have to buy what you need, which you can do either by outright purchase or on hire purchase (if your parent signs the agreement), or if you don't wish to buy, you may be able to lease. If you buy equipment, you must remember that, if you dispose of it, you can only sell it second-hand. In other words, it begins to lose value as soon as you take possession of it. This is known as depreciation and is a charge on your business.

Equipment not only depreciates in value, it depreciates in a real sense: it wears out. It has to be serviced and repaired from time to time, and eventually the moment will come for it to be replaced. Your forward planning must take these facts into account.

Besides equipment, your business will also need some working capital. Money will be needed to buy raw materials, stationery, postage stamps, and to pay National Insurance contributions and the insurance premiums on your property and equipment. You will also need money to pay for your own keep until the business is able to finance you out of the profits.

A lot of expenditure will be necessary when you first set up the business, and you will have other bills coming in as time goes on. They will not all arrive at the same time, nor at the same intervals. So you must include all these demands in your advance plan, and do your best to forecast their amounts and the dates on which payments will fall due.

The following is a list of some of your possible overheads:

- Wages, salaries (if you take on any employees)
- PAYE, VAT
- National Insurance
- Materials
- Capital equipment (direct payment, hire purchase or leasing)
- Postage
- Petrol
- Stationery
- Electricity
- Telephone

- Rent
- Interest on loans

Cash Flow
Having worked out your expenditure over the next year, you must now work out how much income you can expect and when it will come to you. You will probably discover that, although your income by the end of the year is quite enough to meet your expenses, there are times during the year when bills will come in and you will not have sufficient funds to meet them. In other words, during the year you may meet cash flow problems.

Even large businesses suffer from cash flow difficulties and the government itself is no exception. Money from taxation tends to come in to the Chancellor of the Exchequer in one or two big bursts. But the expenses of government have to be met week by week, and there are times when there is not enough money in the national coffers to pay civil service salaries, soldiers' pay, and so on. The government therefore has to do the same as businesses do – borrow.

Unfortunately, you are not the government and may not find borrowing so easy. That is why it is so important to plan your way ahead, and realise in good time (even before you go into business perhaps) when these cash flow problems will arise. You then stand a chance of doing something about them. If you can persuade someone to make you a loan, you will have found one way of dealing with the problem (though, of course, it has to be repaid). Another method is to persuade suppliers to wait a little longer for payment. But bear in mind that cash flow problems have proved fatal for more businesses than one, and can be more serious than lack of profitability.

CANVASSING AND ADVERTISING

Letting the public know you have started a business and getting your first customers are not easy tasks. You have no one to recommend you. Your goods are unknown. The quality of your services has not been tested. People have to take your word for everything.

Once you have been given one or two jobs, or have sold

some of your products, you may be recommended to other customers. If your goods and services are satisfactory you can expect more orders, but even in busy times, you must sustain your marketing efforts. That first breakthrough might take some time to achieve. It may require a lot of hard work, and you may face lots of disappointments.

Ben, for instance, hoped to start work as a self-employed window-cleaner. He had some little cards printed, giving his name and address and setting out his terms. He then called at every house over a wide area, asking the householders whether they were satisfied with their present window-cleaner. He gave his card to everyone he spoke to, and pushed it through the letterbox of every house where he got no reply.

The upshot of all this effort was that he obtained two promises of engagements in two widely separated districts. This was useless, and Ben had to abandon the whole project.

Researching the Market

However, where Ben failed others have been successful. He should have picked a more promising area. Had he sampled only a few houses he would have realised what a hard nut he was trying to crack. He believed that hard work and dogged determination would always pay off, but this is not necessarily true; imaginative foresight and research are much more likely to bring success.

Going around the streets and knocking at doors is not always a bad idea, however, especially if you are not trying to upset long-standing arrangements and you use your initiative. You will remember that it was suggested in Chapter 3 that you take a walk around your own neighbourhood and note down all the little handyman jobs which need doing. If, having done this, you have a word with the various property owners, you stand a very good chance of getting some work. Or you may take a leaf from the book of the girl who arranged a 'cuddly doll party' on the lines of a tupperware party. She knocked on a number of doors in her neighbourhood to invite ladies to attend her party. She provided tea and biscuits, the guests had a pleasant chat, and were able to examine the array of dolls she had made. The resultant sales were most encouraging, and she now intends to persuade her aunt to host a similar party in a different district.

Remember that one job leads to another. So if you get one handyman job to do, keep your eyes open. While you are cleaning out and putting preservative paint on the guttering, see what else needs attention. If you are capable of putting it right, offer to do so. But if it is something which is beyond your skill or knowledge, merely draw attention to it. Explain that it needs a skilled plumber or another craftsman to put it right.

Never try to do things beyond your capabilities; you'll only leave a bad name behind you. However, householders are grateful to be advised about a fault. If you enable them to have repairs done before the damage is serious, they will be very pleased, and your reputation for integrity will have been enhanced.

Publicity

It is useful to have simple business cards printed. They don't need to be elaborate as long as they give your name, address, telephone number, and a brief description of the services you are offering: 'Lawns and verges cut and trimmed; flower beds weeded and tidied; pruning, planting out; care of soil and plants.'

A small advertisement in your local paper is not very expensive and is an excellent way of drawing attention to your business. Even cheaper is an advert in a shop window, which is ideal if you are trying to get work in a small locality. You should also study the advertisements of other people; they may be advertising for the very services you yourself are offering.

One of the most tried and tested methods of advertising – and perhaps the first place people in need of some service think of looking – is in the Yellow Pages. When you subscribe for a business phone, which costs about £80 to have installed, you automatically get an insertion in the Yellow Pages. If you wish for a large, elaborate display entry you can have one if you are prepared to pay extra.

You can advertise in less ostentatious ways, of course. An advert in the church magazine is seldom very costly, and might be very effective because you will probably be known personally to many of the people who see it.

By having a stall or display at a craft fair you can show off your goods and distribute leaflets to enquirers. Even if you fail to make immediate sales you can arouse a lot of interest in this way, and get yourself known among that particular section of the public which is likely to provide you with customers.

If your business involves performing intricate or delicate work, such as lacemaking or painting goose-egg shells, you ought to make sure people actually see you doing it. You might do this in a shop window or at a stall. It is a good idea to have an explanatory notice prominently displayed, perhaps with a photograph of yourself at work.

If you are doing something exceptional, try and get your activities featured in the local (or even the national) newspapers. A headline such as 'Local girl (or Local boy) shows off her (or his) skill' is the sort of advert which is really noticed – and it's free!

HELP AND ADVICE

Being your own boss at 16 usually means starting in a very small way. Most of the help you need will come from your parents and friends. Any professional advice you may require will probably come from the local office of the Department of Social Security, the unemployment benefit office, the office of the local Inspector of Taxes, your local authority, and the Citizens' Advice Bureau.

Accounts

You will need help and advice in keeping accounts, as bookkeeping is an essential part of running a business. You must keep a record of all your transactions, showing where you have spent money, how you have received it, who still owes you, and to whom you yourself are in debt.

Your books will not only tell you how your business is doing and whether you are making a profit or loss, but will enable you to see the areas in which it is doing well and those in which it is doing badly. They will also enable you to make better cash flow forecasts, and help you to decide your future business policy in various ways.

Bookkeeping is also essential for tax purposes. The Inland Revenue will want to know how much money you are making and whether your claims for allowances and expenses are justified. Unless you keep clear accounts and support all your transactions with receipts and invoices, you will end up having trouble with the tax authorities.

When you start your business or begin working as a freelance you should open a cash book and see that you enter all your transactions, day by day. Don't let things pile up. You can buy a suitable book, ready ruled, from any good stationer's. Choose one with several columns in which you can analyse your income and expenditure under various headings. You could have *income* from sale of books, calendars, novelties, confectionery etc (assuming you are running that sort of business) on one side, and *expenditure* on rent, rates, electricity, gas, insurance, NI contributions, postage, telephone, purchase of stock, and payments to self etc, on the other side.

You may not need such detailed analysis. If you are working as a freelance fashion model, for instance, you need only record your income from each engagement and your expenditure on fares, postage and NI contributions, all of which could be entered under the general heading of expenditure.

Further Advice

For more information about bookkeeping you might read the relevant chapters in *Working for Yourself* by Godfrey Golzen (published by Kogan Page). You will find information about such areas as profit and loss accounts and balance sheets, all explained in a straightforward, practical manner. You can, if you so wish, obtain much more detailed books on the subject, meant for professional bookkeeping in large concerns, but you would probably find these more of a hindrance than a help.

One of the things this book wishes to develop is an 'own business' attitude of mind. It assumes, therefore, that having become your own boss at 16, you will continue being your own boss. You may give up one form of business and move into another, but the time should still come when you will need extra capital, when you will engage staff, and eventually you may wish to turn your business into a private limited company.

When that time comes, you will need professional help.

Your bank manager will probably already have recommended an accountant and a solicitor from whom you can obtain specialised advice. You may also obtain help from a number of bodies which have been set up especially to help small businesses. Their addresses are given in Chapter 9, along with a list of other useful books.

Chapter 7

The Financial Side

WHAT DO WE MEAN BY CAPITAL?

Economists tell us that wealth is produced by the *factors of production* working together. These factors are land, labour, capital and enterprise.

They sometimes explain this by taking Robinson Crusoe's island as a model. They point out that in order to get food and clothing, Robinson Crusoe needed:

(a) land on which to grow corn and graze his goats,
(b) capital in the shape of seed and animals,
(c) labour by himself and Man Friday to till the ground and tend the animals,
(d) his own enterprise in organising the whole venture.

All this is very relevant for your business, even if it isn't on a desert island. These factors of production are needed in every business. Even if you become a debt collector, an occupation about as far removed from Crusoe's agricultural pursuits as you can imagine, you must have *land* in the shape of premises to work from; *capital* such as office machinery, stationery, and money to pay for stamps and telephone calls; *labour* to use this equipment and go out and collect the debts; and *enterprise* to have started the business and to keep it going.

Capital is not necessarily money. Money would have been no use as capital to Robinson Crusoe (although for some curious reason he brought some off the wreck). In Chapter 3 we saw that June had founded her theatrical costume business using a collection of costumes as her capital. In other small businesses the capital might consist of a set of ladders, a typewriter, a computer, or a set of carpenters' tools.

The Importance of Saving

It is said that all capital is the result of saving. This is something that would-be small businessmen should note very carefully. If Robinson Crusoe had used all his corn in making flour and not saved some of the seed for planting in the following spring, he would have had no crops the next year. He provided himself with capital by saving. One way or another all businesses have to do the same.

So if you are hoping to start a business and you are wondering where the necessary capital is to come from, the answer is that it has to come from saving. You can begin to do this even while you are at school, putting aside money earned from your paper round, for example, and denying yourself such luxuries as visits to a cinema, a new coat, or a holiday. A newspaper has just carried an account of a school-leaver who has amassed a considerable sum from his paper rounds. He had five of them, and wondered whether he had established a record by delivering over 110,000 papers during his employment.

Although your capital must come from such reserves, it need not be from your own. Thousands of people are saving every week, putting money into savings banks, building societies and National Savings accounts. This all goes to provide capital for other people to use. People who want to buy their homes borrow capital from the building societies; the government, wanting to pay its staff, borrows from the National Savings Department. If you want to borrow money to start a business, you would go to a bank.

Of course, those who have denied themselves the use of their own money have a right to claim some reward from those who use it. The reward they obtain is known as *interest*. So if you are in the process of building up reserves, ready for the day when you hope to set up your own business, you should think of lending them until you are ready to use them. You will then add interest.

You can invest your money in a variety of ways – in Savings Certificates, the National Savings Bank, the Trustee Savings Bank, or in a building society. Some methods give you better rates of interest than others; some are more difficult to get your money from quickly should you require it. So you ought to 'shop around' – there are often articles on saving schemes in the daily papers and in several women's magazines. You should read them, for they will assist you in acquiring the business sense you want.

Borrowing

If you cannot save sufficient money for all your capital needs, you may have to consider borrowing. If your business is to be a simple one – window-cleaning, shall we say – and all you need by way of capital is a ladder, a bucket and a shammy leather, you should be able to borrow the money from your family.

In this respect, it seems that Asian families provide much more help for their junior members than British or Afro–West Indian ones. It is by no means unusual for an Asian family to provide the £1000 and even more for one of their members to set up a business, taking advantage of the Enterprise Allowance Scheme (described on page 105). As was mentioned earlier, they are much more 'own-business minded' than others in the community. What is more, they have learned the simple economic truth that capital is the result of saving, and they put money aside for this purpose. This gives them the edge over other groups who have to go cap in hand to the bank manager when the need for capital arises.

Failing the family, the bank manager is the obvious person to turn to next. Bank managers, however, are not noticeably keen to lend customers' money to very inexperienced school-leavers. They might do so for a pop star (even to one under 18) in special circumstances, but the arrangements might have to be in the name of the star's manager. (See Chapter 5 about the law of contract.) Of course, your parents might be able to help you by borrowing money themselves, and then lending it to you. But they would have to provide the security for the loan.

Credit

Fortunately, there are other ways of borrowing money which avoid going to anyone and asking bluntly for a loan. When you ask someone to give you credit, such as the milkman is usually prepared to do until the end of the week, you are in fact borrowing. If you are a shopkeeper you probably get most of your stock on credit. You may have goods supplied on a sale-or-return basis, too, which is another form of borrowing.

The business world runs on credit. It is the oil which

lubricates business wheels. If traders could not get goods without having to pay for them immediately, most trade would come to a halt.

Often, this form of borrowing is all you need to start a business. Once you have taken delivery of a parcel of goods, for which you will not have to pay for (say) a month, your business can get under way. You will, we assume, have a stall or pitch (the necessary *land*). You have your own *labour* and *enterprise*. The award of credit has given you the *capital*.

Another form of credit is hire purchase. Using this arrangement you can have the use of a piece of equipment, machinery or furniture etc, and pay for it over a period. There are various forms of payment by instalments. Under some agreements ownership of the goods remains with the dealer until all the payments are completed. In others the title is transferred at once to the purchaser. It is a complicated subject, and there are books devoted to it. Given the range of options, it is advisable to take care before entering into any agreement of this nature, so don't sign a contract until you have shown it to someone who understands these matters.

Hiring

This is another way of obtaining the use of capital goods and, again, is just another form of borrowing. In recent years the leasing of equipment has become a widespread activity. Firms such as Rediffusion Ltd have been leasing radios and television sets for a long time, and the introduction of viewdata and video has much increased their business. You will have noticed, too, that much of the equipment used on building sites and civil engineering projects is not the property of the contractors actually doing the work. The cranes, bulldozers and tractors are leased by firms which specialise in providing such equipment.

You may not be aware that a great deal of office equipment is also leased. There are firms which lease computers, word processors, photocopiers, filing cabinets, and so on. It is quite possible to have a complete modern electronic office without actually owning a single item of equipment. Of course, you need some money to pay for the installation and the initial leasing charges, but these will only be a fraction of the cost of the equipment.

Such arrangements are, in general, out of the question for school-leavers, but it is important to recognise the possibilities which lie ahead. For further information about raising capital you should refer to *Working for Yourself* by Godfrey Golzen or one of the other books listed in Chapter 9.

A final point has to be made about borrowing. When you are drawing up an estimate of the future income and expenditure of your business you must not forget to include the cost of borrowing among your liabilities. You may also have to repay a capital sum by instalments.

NATIONAL INSURANCE

A brief mention of your liability to pay National Insurance contributions has been made in the last chapter. When you are self-employed you are responsible for making sure you make these payments. You should make yourself familiar with your responsibilities and entitlements under the National Insurance Acts by going to the local office of the Department of Health and Social Security and asking for the following leaflets:

- NI.41 (April 1985) – National Insurance Guide for the Self-Employed; and
- NI.27A (February 1985) – People with Small Earnings from Self-Employment.

Self-employed persons pay what are known as Class 2 contributions. You may pay these by purchasing DHSS stamps at the current (1985) flat rate of £3.50 weekly from the Post Office. If you don't want to do this (and you can waste a lot of time in Post Office queues) you can arrange for your bank to make the necessary payments by standing order. It is most important that you don't fall behind in these payments. The sum of £3.50 every week may seem quite a burden, but if you get a month in arrears, you will be faced with a bill for £14, and by the end of the year this will have amounted to £182. You may be in desperate straits to find such a sum. So pay week by week, one method or another.

Contributors to Class 2 are not entitled to claim unemployment benefit. They may, however, claim sickness benefit should they fall ill. Class 2 contributions also entitle to maternity grant and allowance, and to a retirement pension.

You will find that the Acts require you in certain circumstances to pay a special contribution known as Class 4. This is paid through the Inland Revenue at the end of the tax year, so you don't have to buy any stamps or make any arrangements with your bank.

Class 4 is not levied at a flat rate. It varies with your annual profits. At present the Inland Revenue demands a payment of 6.3 per cent of your profits if they are between £4,150 and £13,780 in the year (1985 figures).

INCOME TAX

Class 4 NI contributions should not be confused with income tax although they are collected by the Inland Revenue. Even when you have paid Class 4 you are still liable to pay income tax on the income you derive personally from your business.

When you are working on your own account you are not taxed under the Pay As You Earn system (PAYE). So when you start in business you should notify your local Inspector of Taxes and arrange to be taxed under Schedule D. This will enable you to offset your expenses against your gross profits. The Inland Revenue publishes a useful explanatory leaflet called 'Starting in Business'. You should get hold of a copy and read it carefully. You will see the importance of keeping good accounts and preserving your receipts etc.

VALUE ADDED TAX

Value Added Tax (VAT) worries many people who work for themselves. It is a curious tax, because although in the end it is paid by the consumer – that is the person who eventually buys the product for his or her own use – in the course of its production and sale the product can have passed through several hands and all these handlers will have paid some tax on it. Each handler recovers the tax from the person who is the next down the chain. But as with all these schemes it is rather more complicated than that, and requires a lot of bookkeeping.

Only VAT-registered persons are involved in these arrangements. If your turnover is less than £19,500 each year of

£6,500 in a quarter (1985 figures), you are not required to register. Although registration does involve a considerable amount of record-keeping, it has advantages. If you are registered and have paid VAT on plant, machinery, typewriters, stationery etc, you can reclaim the money.

VAT is a very involved subject, and the above account deals only with the theory and not the actual working of the scheme. For full details you should obtain the pamphlet issued by HM Customs and Excise entitled 'Should I be Registered for VAT?'

INSURANCE COVER

You have probably never given much thought to the question of insurance. While you are at school it hardly concerns you. But it is possible that you have insured your bicycle against damage or theft. If you are the owner of a motor-cycle you will have been compelled by law to take out insurance to cover any damage or injury you might cause to other persons. But when you go into business on your own account you must think about insurance very carefully.

If you intend to work from your own home, you may be putting the property at a greater risk than it was before. You may intend to do things which are to some extent hazardous – brazing metal, cooking on a large scale (for a domestic house), storing inflammable materials etc.

Your parents will probably already have the house insured. But your new activities might have added a new element of risk. Remember that contracts of insurance require the utmost good faith. They require such changes in use of a property to be reported at once. This may result in an increased premium, but unless the changes have been reported the insurers may refuse to pay any compensation should a fire or explosion be caused by your activities.

You must also think about your chances of being injured in the job you intend to undertake. If you become a window cleaner, for example, you could easily fall off a ladder. Most occupations have some danger attached to them. Even clerks have been known to be killed when filing cabinets have fallen on them. It is true that there is national provision for such accidents under the Industrial Injuries scheme, but you may wish to ensure you have additional cover.

Even more important is insurance against the chance of your injuring a member of the public in the course of your work. If you are repairing a gutter and you drop a trowel which hits and injures a passer-by, you may be liable to heavy damages. You must be insured against public liability to protect yourself against such claims.

Should the time come when you find yourself having to employ someone to help you, you should take out insurance against your liability as an employer. Your employee may suffer some injury while working for you. He or she might, for example, fall down your badly lit cellar steps, or slip on your polished floor. It is hoped you will take every precaution to make such accidents impossible, but the fact remains that staff do have a number of minor accidents and for some of these you may well be liable.

In this connection, you should keep an accidents book. This should record every accident, however trivial it might seem, with the time and date of its occurrence, and an account of what happened and what treatment was given.

You will also need to insure your stock, and to insure against any consequent loss which the loss of or damage to your stock might cause you.

Finally you must consider what might happen if someone is hurt by something you have made and sold to them. For example, a child may suck poisonous paint from a toy you have made, or an amateur actress contract a skin complaint from a fur coat out of your wardrobe. This is another form of public liability and you should be insured against possible claims.

PROFIT AND LOSS

An American theorist (Peter Drucker) has declared that businesses have two functions. The first is to supply goods and services at a price their customers are prepared to pay. The other is 'to improve and maintain the wealth-producing capacity of the economic resources entrusted to them'.

Many people might argue with this dictum, but it is interesting, and worth bearing in mind. If the first function is neglected, the business will simply fold up. If the second is not acted upon, the business will be pushed aside by energetic competitors. This has been demonstrated by the fate of several traditional British industries. Because they failed to improve and maintain their wealth-producing capacity, they have been overtaken by the Americans or the Japanese. Or, as in the case of the car industry, they have had to be modernised at huge expense and at the cost of a painful upheaval for everyone concerned.

Updating and improving is just as important in a small business as in a large one. If you are running a teashop you must see that it keeps up with the times. It will need redecorating, refurnishing, re-equipping with up-to-date water-heaters, micro-wave ovens etc. Even if you are trying to give a place an 'olde world' atmosphere, you cannot use yesterday's chipped teapots and soot-blackened kettles.

You might have expected that one of the functions quoted above would have been simply 'to make a profit'. Most people, if asked, would reply that that was the end in view for every business. But although this theorist agrees that businesses should aim 'not to make a loss', he avoids any mention of profit.

However, this is not as strange as it may seem, and if you bear these ideas in mind you can ensure that your business will grow and remain healthy. You may ask how you are going to find the means to live if your business doesn't make a profit. The answer, of course, is that your salary is an expense to be borne by your business in the same way as any wage it might pay to one of your employees. You must regard the profit made by the business as the surplus after these expenses have been met.

If there is any profit, you should plough it back into the business and thus improve and maintain the wealth-producing capacity of its resources. You may even be able to reduce the cost of your products and by lowering prices, undercut your competitors.

COSTING

This raises the question of what you should charge for your goods or services. Something has already been said about the 'law' of supply and demand. If you run a vegetable stall you will know how this operates. When the supply of strawberries is limited in early summer, the price is high thus reducing the effective demand for the small amount available. But in midsummer when there is a glut of strawberries, the price comes right down. The aim of traders is now to persuade customers to buy more.

But not all goods are like strawberries and other seasonal commodities. So how do you price an article such as a lady's coat, or a service such as cleaning out a gutter?

You can arrive at an approximate answer by calculating how much such 'goods' have taken to produce. To make a lady's coat, you have to use so many yards of material, so much thread, so many buttons etc. Then there are all sorts of overheads – some fraction of what you pay out for rent, rates, heating, interest on loans, insurance premiums, your own salary, and so on. To clean out a gutter you have to charge some small fraction of the money you spent to buy your ladder and tools. There is the cost of getting to the house where the gutter is to be cleaned; the cost of housing your ladder when it is not in use; your insurance premium, your NI contribution, and your own labour. Some part of all these costs goes to the cost of cleaning out your client's gutter. It might take you quite a while to calculate with any degree of accuracy what this amount is.

You will see that costing is a difficult exercise. You will probably abandon any hope of doing it very scientifically, and be satisfied with some rule of thumb. Having obtained your necessary equipment, you may well forget about the element of capital outlay and replacement of equipment which would figure in a true estimate, and content yourself with charging your client on the basis of how long the job will take. If you are costing a lady's coat you might base it only on the cost of material and your own time.

But if you begin dealing in a number of lines, making a variety of goods, or carrying out several types of service, you may want to work out their cost more exactly. You may need help to do so. Probably the best way to set about it is to study some elementary book on the subject. Your local librarian will help you to find one. As your business grows you may need professional assistance.

Why might you wish to have accurate costing? The obvious answer is that it enables you to know whether you are selling things too cheaply or too dearly. You can then adjust the prices you are charging. It might become clear too that you cannot make some article at a price which your customers are prepared to pay. You will then have to consider whether you should continue producing it. This may not be such an easy decision as it seems. It may be worth your while to sell a particular product at a slight loss if by so doing you can sell others at a good profit. Only good costing can give you the information on which your decision will have to be based.

BANKRUPTCY

This book hopes to inspire you to found a successful business and maintain and expand it. But you may run into difficulties. These may not be your fault. All sorts of things can lead to a business failing. A new shopping centre might lead to the decay of smaller shops and markets. A prolonged strike – such as the miners' strike of 1984–85 – can cripple many small businesses in the area. There might be a change of fashion and leave you with stock which no one wants any more.

As a sole trader you are in a very exposed position. If your liabilities exceed your assets and you go bankrupt, your creditors are entitled to seize and sell all your possessions (personal ones as well as the assets of your business) in order to satisfy your debts.

It hardly needs saying that you must exercise great care to try and ensure you never get into such a situation. Good management, including good bookkeeping, is the first priority. But you need foresight. You have to keep your ear to the ground to know what is going on around you and the imagination to realise what might be the results of developments and their effect upon your business. You need prudence. Don't, for example, buy a larger stock of goods than you can possibly ever sell, just because it is offered to you at a cheaper price per item than a smaller consignment.

But let it be hoped you will not be faced by these difficulties, and that in due course your business will become a limited company in which the shareholders are only liable for the debts of the company to the amount of their shares.

Chapter 8

Assistance for Small Businesses

A young person setting out in business on his or her own account need not feel friendless. The world of business can be difficult and confusing. There are numerous legal obstacles and requirements. There are many things to learn, and awkward choices to be made. But fortunately there are various bodies from which advice can be sought.

It is well worth your while, therefore, when the plans for your possible business are just beginning to take shape in your mind, to discover what agencies etc have been set up in your own area, and to get in touch with them.

You probably know that in most towns there is a Chamber of Commerce or Chamber of Trade. These organisations exist to represent the interests of all the local merchants, traders, manufacturers, bankers and business people. Chambers of Trade are more restricted in their scope, and are made up of retail traders and small businessmen. Both of these bodies may be able to help you, but you are likely to find the Chamber of Trade more attuned to your particular needs. In many towns special centres have been set up, either by the local Chamber of Commerce or the Chamber of Trade to give you the sort of advice you might require.

Some of these *Small Business Advice Centres* even have modest amounts of money available to lend to people starting up. But their main purpose is to put new business-people in touch with the experts who can help them – professional people such as solicitors and accountants. They are also able to link the starter with established firms who can assist them by providing necessary services or in such activities as marketing and advertising.

Business Information Services which are provided by local authorities give specialised advice and assistance in obtaining information. For example, you may wish to know how to obtain supplies of certain materials, or what outlets exist for your particular products. You may be in need of technical information, or of advice on the purchase of suitable plant and equipment. Business Information Services centres can help you obtain such information by making technical books and publications available, and also by giving you access to appropriate data bases.

Enterprise Agencies, under whatever title they might use in your aea, are also very helpful in giving advice, and may be able to offer premises. The London Enterprise Agency even offers one-day courses in 'Build your own business' and holds linked weekend seminars.

The Department of Trade and Industry is naturally interested in giving all possible encouragement to small businesses. After all, in recent years small businesses have been responsible for creating the majority of new jobs. The Department has a special *Small Firms Service* with offices in most parts of the country. It is not really concerned with such very small businesses as those described in Chapter 4, yet it is as well that you should know of these facilities. It is hoped that in time the 'own boss at 16' will need the sort of high-powered advice this service provides. It should be noted that the Department issues a number of free publications on setting up a business. These are worth obtaining (for the address, see Chapter 9).

There are a number of schemes which aim specifically at helping young people under 25. These include two trusts – *The Royal Jubilee Trust* and *The Prince's Trust* – which co-operate in the *Youth Business Initiative* to help unemployed young people to start work on their own account. This is done by providing capital to set up a business and by attaching two advisers to each project. The Youth Business Initiative also has certain funds available to give limited financial assistance to young business-people.

Another scheme is known as *Livewire (England and Wales)*. It does not assist financially, but has set up a network of advisers to help young entrepreneurs.

Two other interesting organisations must be mentioned. *Young Enterprise* is designed for young people still at school or college. It encourages them to become 'own business-minded' by setting up small enterprises while they are still receiving full-time education. The enterprises set up under the scheme are not intended to continue after the participants have left school or college. They are run to teach young people the rudiments of running a business. When the class breaks up, the enterprise normally comes to an end, but there have been cases where they have carried on and actually become viable concerns.

Instant Muscle is the name given to a group of small businesses already started by young people. They are linked by a central controlling body, which also organises a network of consultants who can provide advice to young people wishing to start up.

The Enterprise Allowance Scheme is a government scheme for people over 18 who have been claiming unemployment benefit or supplementary benefit for 13 weeks or more. Although it is not applicable to young people wishing to be their own boss at 16, it is worth knowing that such a scheme exists. It offers £40 per week for up to one year for persons wishing to become self-employed. Applicants have to be able to put up £1,000, either in money or equipment, towards the necessary capital. Help and advice from the Small Firms Service or Jobcentres is available to persons benefiting under the Scheme.

Chapter 9

Further Information

BOOKS TO READ

All Our Own Work by Linda Thompson with the Basic Skills Unit (Careers and Occupational Information Centre – COIC)

Be Your Own Boss: How to Become Self-Employed by John Blundell (National Federation of the Self-Employed)

Be Your Own Boss Kit by D S Watkins and others (National Extension College and Yorkshire Television)

Creating Your Own Work by Micheline Mason (Gresham Books)

Croner's Reference Book for the Self-Employed and Smaller Businesses, edited by Daphne McAra (on subscription only from Croner Publications Ltd)

Getting Sales by Richard D Smith and Ginger Dick (Kogan Page)

Going Solo by William Perry and Derek Jones (BBC Publications)

The Guardian Guide to Running a Small Business, edited by Clive Woodcock (Kogan Page)

How to Survive Unemployment by Robert Nathan and Michael Syrett (Penguin; has a valuable chapter on Creating Your Own Enterprise)

Minding Your Own Business by P Phillips and C Swanson (Careers and Occupational Information Centre – COIC)

The Mini Co Kit by Elizabeth Bray (Longman)

Occupation: Self-Employed by Rosemary Pettit (Wildwood House)

Running Your Own Building Business by Kim Ludman (Kogan Page)

Running Your Own Catering Business by Ursula Garner and Judy Ridgway (Kogan Page; all based on catering from home)

Self-Sufficiency 16–25 by Richard Bourne and Jessica Gould (Kogan Page)

The Small Business Guide by Colin Barrow (BBC Publications)

Work for Yourself: A Guide for Young People by Paddy Hall (National Extension College in association with Shell)

Working for Yourself: The Daily Telegraph Guide to Self-Employment by Godfrey Golzen (Kogan Page)

Writing for a Living by Ian Linton (Kogan Page)

USEFUL ADDRESSES

Council for Small Industries in Rural Areas (CoSIRA)
141 Castle Street, Salisbury, Wiltshire SP1 3TP; phone 0722 336255; and throughout rural England (see Yellow Pages)

Small Firms Centres
(Department of Trade and Industry)
Head Office: Ashdown House, 123 Victoria Street, London SW1E 6RB; phone 01–212 8667; 11 regional offices can be contacted by dialling 100 and asking for Freefone Enterprise.

Northern Ireland Development Agency
100 Belfast Road, Holywood, County Down; phone 02317 4232

Scottish Development Agency
120 Bothwell Street, Glasgow G2 7JP; phone 041–248 2700
and
102 Telford Road, Edinburgh EH4 2NP; phone 031–343 1911

Welsh Development Agency
Treforest Industrial Estate, Pontypridd, Mid Glamorgan CF37 5UT; phone 044 385 2666

Business in the Community
227A City Road, London EC1V 1LX; phone 01–253 3716

Careers and Occupational Information Centre (COIC)
Manpower Services Commission, Moorfoot, Sheffield S1 4PQ; phone 0742 753275
and
5 Kirk Loan, Corstorphine, Edinburgh EH12 7HD; phone 031–334 9821

Croner Publications Ltd
Croner House, 173 Kingston Road, New Maldon, Surrey KT3 3SS; phone 01–942 8966

Education for Enterprise Network
1 Silver Street, Cambridge CB3 9EC

Instant Muscle
c/o Rank Xerox (UK) Ltd, Bridge House, Oxford Road, Uxbridge, Middlesex UB8 1HS; phone 0895 51166

Livewire (England and Wales)
National Extension College, 18 Brooklands Avenue, Cambridge CB2 2HN; phone 0223 316644

London Enterprise Agency
69 Cannon Street, London EC4N 5AB; phone 01–248 4444

National Extension College
(See Livewire above)

National Federation of Self Employed and Small Businesses
32 St Anne's Road West, Lytham St Anne's, Lancashire FY8 1NY; phone 0253 720911

Project North East
Marseilles Chambers, 45 Groat Street, Newcastle upon Tyne NE1 1UG, phone 0632 617856

Royal Jubilee Trust (with The Prince's Trust)
8 Buckingham Street, London WC2N 6BU

Young Enterprise
Robert Hyde House, 48 Bryanston Square, London W1H 7LN; phone 01–723 4070

Practical Action
Victoria Chambers, 16–20 Strutton Ground, London SW1P 2HP; phone 01–222 3351

Youth Aid
9 Poland Street, London W1V 3DG; phone 01–439 8523

Index